NATIONAL BOARD CERTIFICATION IN LIBRARY MEDIA:

A Candidate's Journal

By Peggy Milam, Ed.S.
National Board Certified Library Media Specialist

Linworth Books

Professional Development Resources for
K-12 Library Media and Technology Specialists

Library of Congress Cataloging-in-Publication Data

Milam, Peggy S., 1953-
National board certification for library media: a candidate's journal/
by Peggy Milam.
   p. cm.
 Includes bibliographical references and index.
 ISBN 1-58683-183-6 (pbk.)

1. School librarians—Certification—Standards—United States.
2. Instructional materials personnel—Certification—Standards—United States.
3. Media programs (Education)—United States.
4. School librarians—Diaries. I. Title.
Z682.4.S34M546 2005
020'.92--dc22
                          2005017034

Published by Linworth Publishing, Inc.
480 East Wilson Bridge road, Suite L
Worthington, Ohio 43085

Copyright ©2005 by Linworth Publishing, Inc.

All rights reserved. Reproduction of this book in whole or in parts is prohibited without permission of the publisher.

ISBN 1-58683-183-6

5 4 3 2 1

Table of Contents

Introduction
    Maintain the Status Quo or Grow? 9
    Journal Entry: August 21 10

Chapter 1 — National Board Certification: The Vision 11
    Journal Entry: August 25 12
    How Did the National Board for Professional Teaching Standards Originate? 13
    Who Makes Up the National Board? 13
    Journal Entry: August 30 14
    The National Board Vision 15
    Table 1: Candidate Qualifications 15
    Journal Entry: September 1 16
    The Five Core Propositions 15
    Table 2: The National Board for Professional Teaching Standards' Five Core Propositions ..17
    Journal Entry: September 2 18
    The Library Media Standards 17
    Table 3: The Library Media Standards 21
    Journal Entry: September 4 20
    Uniqueness of National Board Certification Process 21
    Journal Entry: September 5 22
    Evidence of Accomplishment 25
    Table 4: Types of Evidence for Documentation 25
    Journal Entry: September 8 23
    Reflective Practice 25
    Journal Entry: September 12 24
    Table 5: Peggy's List of Helpful Web Sites for National Board Candidates 27
    Journal Entry: September 15 26

Chapter 2 — The Five Core Propositions 29
    What Teachers Should Know and Be Able to Do 31
    Table 6: Mission of the National Board for Professional Teaching Standards 31
    The Wide Influence of National Board Certification 33
    Journal Entry: September 20 32
    Table 7: Comparison of Current Library Media NBCTs by State 33
    Journal Entry: September 23 34
    Explanation of the Five Core Propositions 33
    Journal Entry: September 25 36
    Table 8: The Five Core Propositions and Peggy's Practice 37

Chapter 3 — The National Board Library Media Standards 39
    Journal Entry: October 1 40
    Defining Accomplishment 41

  Table 9: Defining the Accomplished Library Media Specialist 41
  Journal Entry: October 2 42
  Table 10: National Board Library Media Standards and Peggy's Practice 44
  Journal Entry: October 3 43
  Table 11: Log of Community Interactions 46

Chapter 4 — Time Management and Organizational Tips 47
  Journal Entry: October 20 48
  Overview of the Process 49
  Journal Entry: October 25 50
  Average Time Commitment 49
  Organizing the Portfolio Instructions 51
  Journal Entry: October 28 52
  Table 12: Quick Tips for Organizing the Portfolio Instructions 51
  Strategic Planning 51
  Timesaving Tips 51
  Table 13: Schedule of Events for Certificate Completion 53

Chapter 5 — Obtaining Support 55
  Journal Entry: October 31 56
  Mentors 57
  Table 14: Peggy's List of Proofreaders 57
  State-Based Incentives 57
  Table 15: Financial Information for Candidates 58
  National Board Academies 58
  E-mail Lists 58
  Publications 58
  Table 16: Online Sources of Support for Candidates 59
  Applying for Candidacy 59

Chapter 6 — Producing Quality Videotapes 61
  Journal Entry: November 2 62
  Videotaping Entries 63
  Table 17: General Videotape Requirements 63
  Producing Quality Videotapes 63
  Journal Entry: November 5 64
  Planning Portfolio Entries with Videotape Segments 63
  Journal Entry: November 10 66
  Journal Entry: November 15 67
  Seating Students for Videotaping 65
  Journal Entry: November 20 68
  Improving Lighting for Videotaping 65
  Improving Sound Quality for Videotaping 65
  Table 18: Videotaping Tips from the Pros 69
  Journal Entry: November 23 70
  Assessing Your Own Videotapes 69
  Table 19: Self-Scoring Rubric for Videotapes 71

Chapter 7 — Scoring Rubrics and Assessment Tips ... 73
Journal Entry: December 15 ... 74
Overview of the Scoring Process ... 75
What Matters in Scoring ... 75
Journal Entry: December 20 ... 76
Who Are the Assessors? ... 77
Table 20: Qualifications for Becoming an Assessor ... 77
Assessor Training ... 79
Table 21: Training Sessions for Assessors ... 79
Incentives for National Board Assessors ... 79
Journal Entry: December 30 ... 78
Scoring Rubrics ... 79
How to Estimate Your Scores ... 80
Assessment Tips ... 81

Chapter 8 — Portfolio Writing Styles ... 83
Journal Entry: January 1 ... 84
Portfolio Entries for the Library Media Certificate Field ... 85
Journal Entry: January 5 ... 86
National Board Writing Styles ... 85
Analytical Writing ... 87
Tips for Better Analytical Writing ... 87
Descriptive Writing ... 87
Tips for Better Descriptive Writing ... 87
Reflective Writing ... 89
Tips for Better Reflective Writing ... 89
Journal Entry: January 7 ... 88
Table 22: Portfolio Writing Styles ... 89
Table 23: Tips for Improving Written Entries ... 90

Chapter 9 — Portfolio Entry 1: Instructional Collaboration ... 91
Journal Entry: January 8 ... 92
Entry 1: Instructional Collaboration ... 93
Journal Entry: January 9 ... 94
Library Media Standards Related to Entry 1 ... 95
What Counts in This Entry ... 95
Documenting Collaboration ... 97
Table 24: Collaborative Planning Sheet ... 97
Journal Entry: January 10 ... 96
Analyzing Student Work ... 98
Table 25: Points to Consider in Analyzing Student Work ... 98
Reflection on Instructional Collaboration ... 99
Table 26: Helpful Resources for Entry 1 ... 99
Self-Scoring Rubric for Entry 1 ... 100

Chapter 10 — Portfolio Entry 2: Appreciation of Literature 101
    Journal Entry: January 20 102
    Library Media Standards Related to Entry 2 103
    What Counts in Entry 2 103
    Journal Entry: January 30 104
    Table 27: Brainstorming for Ways to Stimulate Student Appreciation of Literature 105
    Table 28: Helpful Resources for Entry 2 106
    Self-Scoring Rubric for Entry 2 107

Chapter 11 — Portfolio Entry 3: Integrating Technology 109
    Journal Entry: February 2 110
    Library Media Standards Related to Entry 3 111
    What Counts in Entry 3 111
    Journal Entry: February 5 112
    Instructional Materials 113
    Table 29: Brainstorming for Technologies to Incorporate into a Lesson for Entry 3 113
    Journal Entry: February 15 114
    Table 30: Brainstorming for Student Technology Projects for Entry 3 115
    Table 31: Helpful Resources for Entry 3 115
    Self-Scoring Rubric for Entry 3 116

Chapter 12 — Portfolio Entry 4: Documented Accomplishments 117
    Journal Entry: February 22 118
    Library Media Standards Related to Entry 4 119
    What Counts in Entry 4 119
    Journal Entry: February 25 120
    What is an Accomplishment? 119
    What Accomplishments Count? 121
    Table 32: Brainstorming for Types of Accomplishments that Link to Student Achievement .121
    Linking to Student Achievement 123
    What Documents Matter? 123
    Description and Analysis of Accomplishments 123
    Journal Entry: March 3 122
    How to Reflect on Accomplishments 123
    Table 33: Helpful Resources for Entry 4 124
    Self-Scoring Rubric for Entry 4 125

Chapter 13 — Online Assessment Tips 127
    Journal Entry: April 5 128
    Overview of the Online Assessment 129
    Journal Entry: April 10 130
    Assessment Center Tips 129
    How to Study for the Online Assessment 131
    Table 34: Assessment Center KWL 132
    Helpful Resources for the Online Assessment 133

Chapter 14 — After Scores Are Announced, Then What? 137
Journal Entry: November 23 138
When Will Scores Be Announced? 139
Suppose a Candidate Does Not Achieve Certification? 139
Journal Entry: November 30 140
Benefits of Achieving National Board Certification 141
Journal Entry: September 2 142
Educational Honor Society 141
Journal Entry: November 15 143
Continued Professional Growth 141
Ethics for NBCTs 144

Appendices 145
Appendix A: Peggy's Personal Glossary of Terms for National Board Candidates 146
Appendix B: Resource List 147
Appendix C: Index 149

> "A turn in the road is not the end of the road
> unless you fail to make the turn."
> —John M. Capozzi

Introduction

Maintain the Status Quo or Grow?

After twenty-two years of teaching, I had begun to wonder if I was truly making a difference in student achievement. As I listened to reports of budget cuts and job losses nationwide, I wondered what my next performance review might say. I worried about the comments from my coworkers who grumbled that I didn't have papers to grade and parent conferences. I was beginning to lose satisfaction with my job and with my role as a vital member of our learning community.

I began to look at other media specialists who were making a difference. I attended conferences and read professional publications. Although the national research indicated that school library media specialists were a critical part of student achievement, locally no one seemed to take notice. I decided that I needed to show the importance of my position by making a visible difference in my own school. I chose to accept the challenge to grow professionally and embarked on the greatest professional development experience of my life. I began to pursue National Board Certification in Library Media.

This book is the story of my candidacy, from the steps I took before I applied to become a candidate to the day I found out my scores. The book features entries from my journal with supporting details that explain and enhance my journal notes. I have included tips I learned through obtaining National Board certification myself. I discuss scoring from my perspective as a trained National Board assessor in library media. In addition, I offer examples of best practices and include examples of all three writing styles required in the portfolio with an emphasis on reflective writing as a tool to improve practice. While there are many paths to certification, this book describes my journey. Candidates must realize that the activities I detail represent my practice and do not represent the best or only way to achieve certification. There is no template for success; rather, the National Board Certification process is designed to identify best practices in the library media field that are certifiable.

This book will appeal not only to practicing school library media specialists, but also to administrators and support personnel who want to know what the process is all about; moreover, it will appeal to professors in schools of education and library media certification programs nationwide. It will also appeal to boards of education and state department officials who are interested in encouraging state and local employees to obtain National Board Certification.

No such manual for library media specialists exists at this time, although the certification process is gaining in popularity and the number of candidates has increased geometrically each year. At the time of this writing, 1,089 media specialists nationwide are National Board Certified, but the number grows each year.

August 21

It is the start of another school year, but I suspect this year will be very different from any other so far! I have been reading and studying about the National Board vision for accomplished teaching and what is required to become National Board Certified, and I am accepting the challenge. I believe that I need to make a difference personally as well as professionally. I need to show that what I do makes a difference in student achievement. Although I think the research from the school library impact studies is very significant, I also think I need to bring the research closer to home. I want to show that what I do every day in my media center can improve student achievement, too. I have heard about National Board Certification and how it can identify "accomplished" teachers. Once I learn all about it, I am beginning the National Board Certification process myself. I hope I am up to it!

Chapter One

NATIONAL BOARD CERTIFICATION:

The Vision

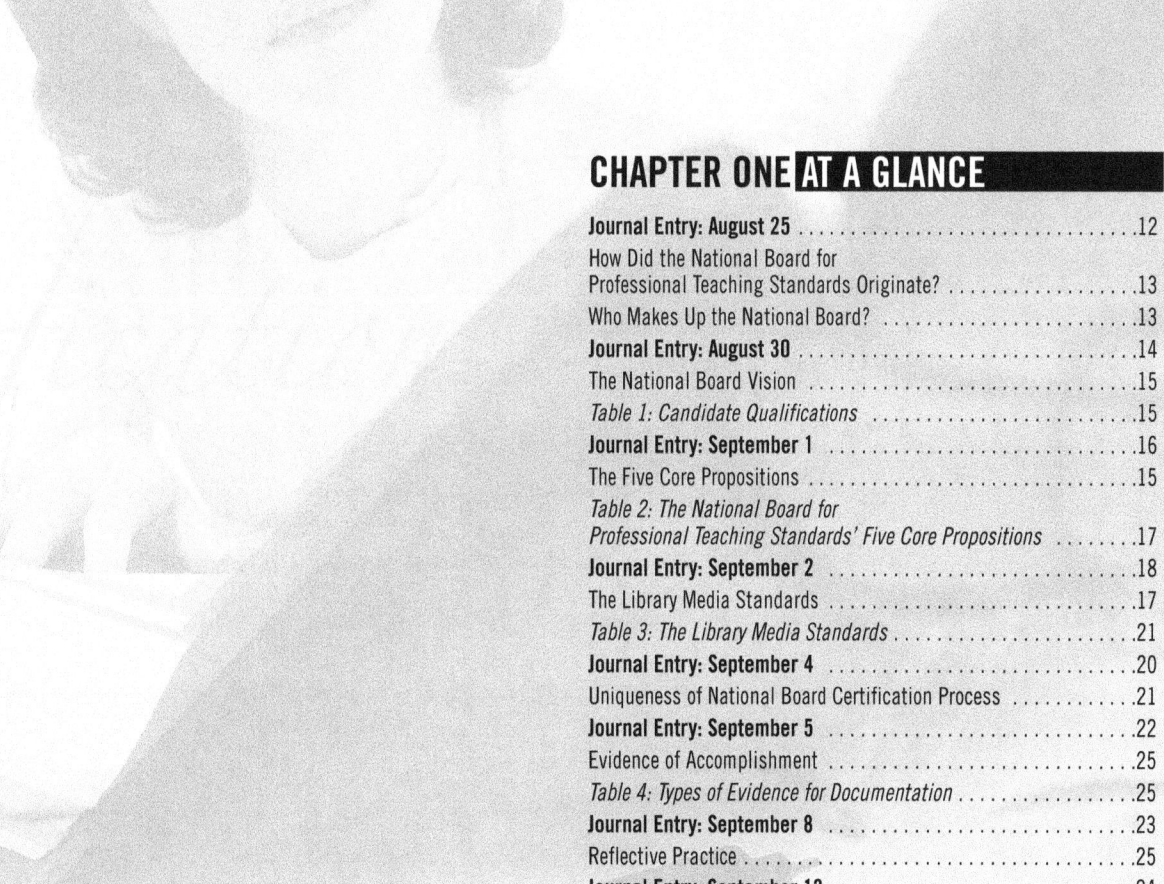

CHAPTER ONE AT A GLANCE

Journal Entry: August 25	12
How Did the National Board for Professional Teaching Standards Originate?	13
Who Makes Up the National Board?	13
Journal Entry: August 30	14
The National Board Vision	15
Table 1: Candidate Qualifications	15
Journal Entry: September 1	16
The Five Core Propositions	15
Table 2: The National Board for Professional Teaching Standards' Five Core Propositions	17
Journal Entry: September 2	18
The Library Media Standards	17
Table 3: The Library Media Standards	21
Journal Entry: September 4	20
Uniqueness of National Board Certification Process	21
Journal Entry: September 5	22
Evidence of Accomplishment	25
Table 4: Types of Evidence for Documentation	25
Journal Entry: September 8	23
Reflective Practice	25
Journal Entry: September 12	24
Table 5: Peggy's List of Helpful Web Sites for National Board Candidates	27
Journal Entry: September 15	26

11

August 25

Oh my goodness—I am tossing and turning and staying awake at night again, scared and worried that by pursuing National Board Certification I am making a big mistake. How can I know if it is a mistake before I try, though? I really want to achieve National Board Certification in Library Media. I feel it is important not only for me, personally, but for my school and my colleagues.

Speaking of colleagues, some of my friends have been asking why I am interested in National Board Certification. I don't really know enough about it yet to give them any background information. All I know right now is that I want to get certified, whatever it takes. My friends thought that saying I felt driven to go for it was a pretty lame reason. Maybe they don't understand my motivation to reinvent myself and to make a statement for my profession.

I guess if I am going to invest my time and money in this, I really should investigate it pretty thoroughly. I don't want to make a decision based on poor information. That certainly doesn't exemplify an information literate person, does it? There must be some research out there on National Board candidates and their experiences. My current understanding is that National Board Certification in Library Media is a relatively new field. I will see what I can find out about it.

> *"If you keep doing what you're doing, you'll keep getting what you're getting."*
>
> —Stephanie Knobel

How Did the National Board for Professional Teaching Standards Originate?

In 1983, the landmark report, "A Nation at Risk," set off alarms nationwide by claiming that the state of American education was, at best, mediocre, and was failing to keep pace with the changing global society. In response to these alarms, the Carnegie Task Force followed with the 1986 report, "A Nation Prepared: Teachers for the 21st Century," which urged the profession to redesign our schools through the teaching staff by forming an agency entitled the National Board for Professional Teaching Standards, whose task it was to create the benchmarks denoting accomplished teaching. The plan was to retain, reward, and advance those teachers whose professional practice reflected these standards consistently.

Fast Fact:
Read about the Carnegie Task Force online at *http://www.nbpts.org/about/hist.cfm#taskforce*.

Who Makes Up the National Board?

The National Board is an organization of administrators, school board leaders, business and community leaders, and classroom teachers. It is independent, nonprofit, and nonpartisan. It has attained broad support from government officials, and from many other organizations such as the National Council for Accreditation of Teacher Education, The American Federation of Teachers, the National Education Association, The National School Boards Association, the National Alliance of Black School Educators, and so on. Support has also come from foundations, corporations, and private enterprises including the Carnegie Corporation, The DeWitt Wallace-Reader's Digest Fund, State Farm Insurance Companies, Xerox, AT&T, Proctor and Gamble, and many others. The Educational Testing Service, Inc. and Harcourt Educational Management monitor the scoring process and collect statistics on its credibility and accuracy.

Fast Fact:
Read about the constitution of the National Board online at *http://www.nbpts.org/about/dir.cfm*.

August 30

If the National Board for Professional Teaching Standards was designed to recognize accomplished teaching, I need to define exactly what accomplished teaching is. I think accomplishment means teaching that excels, but it is difficult to define "excels." Does that mean to excel in methodology, pedagogy, or what? I am sure there must be a connection to student achievement somewhere. I guess I am going to have to determine what the National Board considers to be accomplished teaching.

Since certification in library media is a new certificate field, I don't know any other media specialists who are National Board Certified. Perhaps I can find some coworkers who are National Board Certified in other fields and discuss accomplishment with them. Surely they can identify what constitutes accomplishment in the field. Could there be some video samples of accomplished teaching somewhere? Hmmm, I will have to check on that idea.

In the meantime, I am wondering what I am currently doing on the job that might represent "accomplished" teaching and what things I am doing now that I might need to do differently if I am going to achieve my goal of becoming National Board Certified. I realize that no one is going to do this for me. I also realize that I need to align my practice with the National Board vision of accomplishment and the mission of the National Board. I think if I can get a good grasp on these two things, I will be on my way to focusing my efforts toward achieving my goal.

The National Board Vision

The vision of the National Board for Professional Teaching Standards is to "retain, reward and advance accomplished teachers through a system of advanced certification." While state boards of education set the minimum standards for teachers to become certified in that state, the National Board has defined rigorous standards of professionalism for teachers, and has initiated a voluntary certification process to identify teachers whose practice exemplifies the National Board vision for accomplished teaching. National Board Certification® is the highest degree of certification awarded nationwide to certified professionals with three or more years of experience who are accomplished in their field.

Fast Fact:

Read about the National Board Vision for Accomplished Teaching online at http://www.nbpts.org/standards/nbcert.cfm#stdsgeninfo.

What Qualifications Must a Candidate Meet?

Table 1

Candidate Qualifications

Candidates for National Board Certification must:
- *Possess a baccalaureate degree from an accredited institution.*
- *Have completed three years teaching in their field in a K-12 school.*
- *Have held a valid state license for all three years.*

Potential candidates will be required to submit an eligibility verification packet that includes an education verification form, an employment verification form, and a license verification form (if licensing is required by your state). The initial nonrefundable application fee for candidates is $300. The entire certification process costs $2,300.

Fast Fact:

*Read about the qualifications for candidacy online at **http://www.nbpts.org/candidates/index.cfm#2**.*

The Five Core Propositions

At the root of the vision for National Board Certification are the Five Core Propositions that describe the knowledge, skills, and dispositions that the National Board believes define accomplished teaching. These standards were developed by teachers, with teachers, and for teachers, and are based on the 1989 policy statement, "What Teachers Should Know and Be Able to Do."

September 1

Gosh, I didn't give much thought to whether or not I would qualify for National Board candidacy and what I would have to do to verify my eligibility! Of course I am practicing in the library media field and I am state certified, but it was a long time ago when I got my baccalaureate and even my two masters' degrees. I'll have to look up the address of my colleges on the Internet, I guess. I am sure the transcripts office has changed since I attended classes on either campus. Plus, I have changed jobs several times since graduation. I will need to locate the Human Resources Department of my previous employers. I will have to verify my employment in previous districts as well as my current school district, since I have been at my present position less than three years.

Hmmm, I better get started on writing transcript requests and documenting my credentials. That brings something else to mind: I think I need to start documenting lots of things I have achieved and lots of things I do every day. I can see the need to search through lots of old files. I hope I have the paperwork filed properly. I am going to create some new files for National Board just to keep track of all the documents I need.

Table 2: The National Board for Professional Teaching Standards Five Core Propositions

- *Teachers are committed to students and their learning.*
- *Teachers know the subjects they teach and how to teach those subjects to students.*
- *Teachers are responsible for managing and monitoring student learning.*
- *Teachers think systematically about their practice and learn from experience.*
- *Teachers are members of learning communities.*

Reprinted with permission from the National Board for Professional Teaching Standards, "What Teachers Should Know and Be Able to Do," www.nbpts.org. All rights reserved.

Fast Fact:
Read more about the Five Core Propositions online at *http://www.nbpts.org/about/coreprops.cfm*.

The Library Media Standards

These five core propositions are broken down specifically for each certification area. Standards in each certificate field are developed by teams of teachers, experts, and others with related careers in that field. While under development, each of the standards are open for public examination and then go through extensive revision before finally being approved for that field. The standards in each field should not only reflect the five core propositions, but should also reflect the highest level of knowledge and exemplary practice in that field, as they become the basis for National Board Certification in that certificate area.

In the Library Media field, the ten specific standards are divided into three categories:

- *What media specialists know.*
- *What media specialists do.*
- *How media specialists grow as professionals.*

These standards apply to media specialists who teach students ages 3 to 18+, who have knowledge of information literacy, who practice instructional collaboration, and who integrate technology into their programs.

September 2

I'm getting it! I think the National Board has put into words what all dedicated teachers know deep down inside—that at the heart of good teaching is, first of all, a wealth of knowledge that teachers can translate into words and activities all kids can understand, and, second, that good teachers make an effort to rethink procedures that aren't working to benefit students, and, finally, that behind every good teacher is a strong support system made up of other teachers, parents, and community members. Best of all, I believe I am doing these things. The trick is going to be proving that I am doing them, since the National Board requires "clear, consistent, and convincing evidence" of these signs of accomplishment.

I especially value Standard #7, "Accomplished library media specialists engage in reflective practice to increase their effectiveness." Reflection is something I have been doing unconsciously. Now I find that I need to pay attention to my reflective thoughts as they direct my planning and ultimately, the success of my practice. Reflecting on the National Board's vision of accomplishment has made me consider more deeply the things I value about my job. It is important to me to continue learning about best practices and new research in my field so that I can translate these ideas into action. I like to continue to learn and enjoy modeling lifelong learning for my co-workers and students.

I also know how important it is to have a network of teachers, parents, and community members that form my support system. After all, it is true that it takes a village to raise a child. I think my coworkers know this and that, instinctively, our parents and our community know it, too. We are lucky to have the partners in education that we have and we are beginning to see more parents get involved when they know how they can help. I hope to recruit some volunteers in the media center. I have two faithful parents now. I am going to see what I can do to encourage more parents to join us soon.

I wonder how I can prove these exciting things are happening in my media center? Should I photograph my parent volunteers? Perhaps I should write up an award certificate to give to them. What about our connection to the local bookstores? Maybe a letter from the students thanking them for their contributions would do. Documenting these things will take some careful thought and some work! Note to self: keep copies of everything—you never know when they might come in handy. In this case, I may have to figure out a creative way to document community involvement and networking.

September 4

Today I came across an idea: I printed out the ten standards for library media specialists in large, bold text and posted them on the wall behind my computer monitor where I am always looking at them and am constantly reminded of them. I printed one standard per page and tacked each page to a giant bulletin board behind my computer monitor. Having the standards there in front of me helps me to focus on my goal! It has also led me to think carefully about some of the things I do routinely to see if they reflect the standards.

One of the standards I am not too sure about is #10, "Accomplished library media specialists advocate for the library media program, involving the greater community—" to what "community" does that refer, I wonder? Is it the professional learning community within my school, the community of families, businesses and industries within my cluster of elementary, middle, and high schools, the community of schools within my district, or the community of professional educators within my region? I will need to investigate the definition of community.

Also, I am wondering about Standard #7: "Accomplished library media specialists engage in reflective practice to increase their effectiveness." I already practice reflection, but I wonder what kind of reflection is involved in the portfolio entries: journal writing, e-mail list discussions, sharing e-mail with colleagues? I will need to find that out, as well.

Table 3: The Library Media Standards

- *Accomplished library media specialists have knowledge of learning styles and of human growth and development.*
- *Accomplished library media specialists know the principles of teaching and learning that contribute to an active learning environment.*
- *Accomplished library media specialists know the principles of library and information studies needed to create effective, integrated library media programs.*
- *Accomplished library media specialists integrate information literacy through collaboration, planning, implementation, and assessment of learning.*
- *Accomplished library media specialists lead in providing effective use of technologies and innovations.*
- *Accomplished library media specialists plan, develop, implement, manage, and evaluate library media programs to ensure that students and staff use ideas and information effectively.*
- *Accomplished library media specialists engage in reflective practice to increase their effectiveness.*
- *Accomplished library media specialists model a strong commitment to lifelong learning and to their profession.*
- *Accomplished library media specialists uphold professional ethics and promote equity and diversity.*
- *Accomplished library media specialists advocate for the library media program involving the greater community.*

Reprinted with permission from the National Board for Professional Teaching Standards, Library Media Standards. www.nbpts.org. All rights reserved.

Fast Fact:
Read more about the Library Media Standards online at
http://www.nbpts.org/candidates/guide/whichcert/24EarlyChildYoungLibMedia.html.

Uniqueness of National Board Certification Process

The National Board certification process is unique in that it not only measures the knowledge teachers have about their field, but it also measures how effective they are at communicating that knowledge to their students. This assessment process is inherently complex and involves many examples of accomplished teaching from written essays, to videotapes, to student work samples, to responses to timed test questions. The idea of the National Board Certification process is to examine as many aspects of a teacher's practice as possible to get a broad picture of how a candidate measures up to the standards for that field. Of course, teaching conditions and students vary from one region to another, so the broad sampling helps to level the playing field while still maintaining high and rigorous expectations.

September 5

I have looked closely at what I am already doing that might be considered "accomplished." After researching a bit, I realized that one important practice of accomplished teachers is networking with other professionals—building a sort of support system for sharing ideas and seeking advice. This exemplifies Standard #10—involving the greater community.

As do many library media specialists at the elementary level, I generally work alone in a building and sometimes don't even have a library paraprofessional or a media clerk. I know I don't have a support system in place, so I have decided to join an e-mail list for National Board candidates through Yahoo® groups (www.librarymedia@yahoogroups.com) and am saving pertinent e-mail tips from the group in folders related to the different requirements for certification.

From what I understand from reading the posts so far, there are four portfolio entries, so I have made a folder for tips on each one. I also set up a miscellaneous folder for tips that don't pertain to any specific entry. I am copying and pasting the best ideas from the e-mail list into these folders for future reference. I think I need to read the archives on this e-mail list and save tips from those posts, too. From what I have seen so far, the archives contain comments from other library media specialists who have since become certified.

My mind is spinning with ideas right now, although I am not sure yet which ideas I might need to use.

September 8

Wow, this is awesome! I just read through the entire National Education Association's candidate's guidebook (available online at http://www.nea.org/nationalboard/images/04-05nbcguide.pdf) and am jotting down ideas, notes, and an outline on the four portfolio entries. This document was especially written for teachers who are interested in pursuing National Board Certification and contains a lot of good tips.

I have printed out the whole NEA document, punched three holes in each page, and put the entire guide into a notebook along with my other resources.

Now I have a huge bulletin board with the standards posted, a notebook of ideas, and lots of files. I need to organize all this stuff! Meanwhile, my folders of research are growing. I think I will get a rolling file cart so I can organize my materials and keep everything at hand near my computer.

September 12

I am collecting documents from the Internet and articles from magazines and journals that relate to the four portfolio entries for library media. I spent some time today filing them in the folders I created for my tips. I am also adding in notes and ideas on each entry. I hope I will be well prepared going into the certification process. At least I will have thoroughly researched the library media field! I am making a list of all the Web sites I have found to be helpful so that I can pass this on to others in my support group on the e-mail list. Also, I suspect I might be referring to them a lot as I go along, to be sure that I am on the right track and that I have a clear understanding of the expectations for each entry.

Evidence of Accomplishment

Candidates in all fields are required to submit a portfolio consisting of several different entries demonstrating evidence of that teacher's accomplishment and reflection on his or her practice. Some portfolio entries require candidates to submit student work samples, while other entries may require videotapes of lessons and interactions with students. Additional artifacts such as awards, letters from parents, degrees attained, newspaper articles, and other publications may also be required. In the library media field, candidates must submit portfolio entries in the following four areas: instructional collaboration, literature appreciation, integrating technology, and documented accomplishments.

Table 4

Types of Evidence for Documentation

Entry 1: Instructional Collaboration
   Written commentary
   Student work samples

Entry 2: Literature Appreciation
   Written commentary
   Two-part videotape, up to four documents that further explain the lesson in the videotape

Entry 3: Integrating Technology
   Written commentary
   Two-part videotape

Entry 4: Documented Accomplishments
   Written commentary
   Up to 20 pages of documents such as certificates, letters, transcripts, publications, awards, and so on

---

Fast Fact:
Read more about documenting accomplishments online at
http://www.nbpts.org/candidates/guide/04port/04_ecyalm_instructions/04_ecya_lm_entry4.pd.

Reflective Practice

Not only are candidates required to document evidence that their teaching practice meets or exceeds the established standards for the field, but candidates are also required to systematically analyze and reflect on their practice. Written reflections should give insight into why specific activities were planned and what the goals for each lesson were as well as how the activities were assessed and whether or not students attained the expected outcomes. If students did not attain the expected outcomes, candidates are expected to explain what they might have done differently in order to achieve those goals.

This type of reflective practice is designed to help professional library media specialists create instructional activities that are most effective in meeting the needs of their students and to think carefully about revising activities that are not as successful as originally hoped. This systematic reflection is at the heart of accomplished teaching and is the basis for improving the quality of instruction for all students.

September 15

I am going to search for other candidates in my area so we can form a local support group for National Board Candidates. I found two other media specialists in my district who are pursuing National Board Certification. I wonder if they will be interested in meeting together. Also, I recently heard from my friend who teaches gifted students in a neighboring school district. She is also going through National Board Certification! We are going to stay in touch while we go through this process together. At the very least, we can encourage one another. Plus, it may be helpful to see how she and others are progressing with this so I can pace myself and try to stay on target with writing my entries.

I am also trying to search for mentors. I have asked professors in two different Library and Instructional Technology graduate programs to read and comment on my entries. I have also asked a technology integration specialist in our district Media Services Department to read an entry. I am asking a fellow candidate in another certification field to read an entry for clarity and focus. I am probably going to need all the help I can get on this.

Table 5: Peggy's List of Helpful Web Sites for National Board Candidates

- *National Board Certification: Be sure to visit the sections on standards, certification process, portfolio, and assessment.*
  www.nbpts.org

- *National Education Association National Board for Professional Teaching Standards Candidate Guide: Excellent! I printed this and put it into a notebook.*
  www.nea.org/nationalboard/images/2005-nbc-guide.pdf

- *National Board Candidates Writing Tips.*
  www.coe.ilstu.edu/ilnbpts/NBCT/PreCandidacy/PreCandidacyCourse.htm

- *Librariana: This site is a listing of pertinent Web sites for the practicing librarian. Includes everything from academia to young adults with a brief description of each entry.*
  www.digital-librarian.com/librariana.html

- *American Library Association: Be sure to search the research section and visit the freedom to read and bill of rights statements.*
  www.ala.org/ala/oif/statementspols/ftrstatement/freedomreadstatement.htm
  www.ala.org/ala/oif/statementspols/statements/statementsif/librarybillrights.htm

- *School Library Journal online: Search the archives for full-text articles relating to all categories of assessment.*
  www.slj.com

- *In Focus guide to video production: Excellent! I printed out every section and put them into a notebook for easy reference.*
  www.focusinfo.com/support/articles/vedit.htm
  www.focusinfo.com/articles/vqual.htm

- *National Board for Professional Teaching Standards Video Production 101 Tutorial from the California Arts Project.*
  http://csmp.ucop.edu/tcap/nbpts/tutorials/video.html

- *Lesson plan ideas for collaboration projects.*
  http://www.education-world.com/a_lesson

- *Ideas for incorporating standards into collaborative projects: NCSS thematic standards lessons. Lessons:*
  http://www.socialstudies.org/standards/teachers/vol3/examples

- *Source of integrating technology into interdisciplinary activities.*
  http://www.gpb.org/media/pdf/GPB_1plan.pdf

- *Rubrics: Great source for assessment resources.*
  http://www.teach-nology.com/web_tools/rubrics/

Chapter Two

THE FIVE CORE
Propositions

CHAPTER TWO AT A GLANCE

What Teachers Should Know and Be Able to Do 31
*Table 6: Mission of the National Board for
  Professional Teaching Standards* 31
The Wide Influence of National Board Certification 33
Journal Entry: September 20 32
Table 7: Comparison of Current Library Media NBCTs by State 33
Journal Entry: September 23 34
Explanation of the Five Core Propositions .33
Journal Entry: September 25 36
Table 8: The Five Core Propositions and Peggy's Practice 37

> *"If it's to be, it's up to me!"*
> —Jim Clemmer

What Teachers Should Know and Be Able to Do

The National Board for Professional Teaching Standards was formed in 1987 in response to the Carnegie Task Force report entitled, "A Nation Prepared: Teachers for the 21st Century." The Carnegie task force offered solutions to the "education crisis" identified in the landmark report, "A Nation at Risk." One of the solutions suggested was to establish standards for the profession and then identify teachers who met those standards. The mission of the National Board for Professional Teaching Standards, then, was to establish benchmarks for measuring accomplished teaching practices, certify those teachers who meet the standards, and advocate for educational reform by capitalizing on the expertise of accomplished teachers.

Fast Fact:
Read more about the Carnegie Task Force online at **http://www.nbpts.org/about/hist.cfm#taskforce**.

Table 6

Mission of the National Board for Professional Teaching Standards
- *Maintain high and rigorous standards for what accomplished teachers should know and be able to do.*
- *Provide a national voluntary system certifying teachers who meet those standards.*
- *Advocate related education reforms to integrate National Board Certification in American education and to capitalize on the expertise of National Board Certified teachers.*

Fast Fact:
Read more about the mission of the National Board online at **http://www.nbpts.org/about/hist.cfm**.

The idea was that the influence of National Board Certified teachers would begin a reform movement that would improve education by improving the teaching force. And the force is gaining in strength! According to the National Board Web site (http://www.nbpts.org/nbct/nbctdir_byyear.cfm), as of this writing, approximately 40,206 teachers nationwide have achieved certification. Such numbers make a powerful statement and give greater credence to the mission of the National Board for Professional Teaching Standards.

September 20

Wow, now that I know more about it, I am beginning to see the wide influence of the National Board for Professional Teaching Standards. The course objectives for my Ed.S. program at the university are written so that they reflect the National Board standards. Having course objectives reflecting the standards not only shows the power of the National Board reform effort, but it also works to improve the quality of instruction whether or not the graduate students in the university program ever qualify as candidates.

Staff development courses are offered in my school district to inform teachers about the rigors and benefits of becoming National Board Certified. Our district recognizes candidates who obtain certification and rewards them with an annual bonus check as well.

Our state professional standards commission has added links to the National Board Web site (www.nbpts.org) on its Web site. And, each year, the state professional standards commission hosts a conference for candidates and National Board Certified Teachers throughout our state. The conference not only serves to help candidates locate mentors and network with NBCTs, but it also keeps NBCTs focused on the critical issues in education and ways in which they can continue to share their expertise with others.

Also, I found out that local colleges are offering a course to prepare candidates, and, if I complete the course, I can get a portion of my candidate fees paid by my state! The course is free and online, too! I'm registering for the Knowledgeable Teacher Course right away.

The Wide Influence of National Board Certification

At the heart of the mission of the National Board for Professional Teaching Standards is its belief that education reform lies with the teaching force. According to the National Board Web site (www.nbpts.org), "… the single most important action the nation can take to improve schools and student learning is to strengthen teaching." But how are teachers supposed to improve if they don't know what constitutes exceptionality in teaching practice? This is where the standards come in, but more importantly, where the influence of National Board Certified Teachers comes into play. The impact of these certified teachers is already evident in classrooms nationwide and the movement is spreading. The first school year that certification in Library Media became available, 2001-2002, approximately 800 candidates applied (www.nbpts.org). Those numbers are expected to increase every year as more and more library media specialists achieve certification. Three library media specialists in my district achieved certification in 2002-2003, and at least that many more are expected to achieve certification every year. Each library media specialist who becomes certified can lead additional library media specialists to become certified, and so on. The more certified library media specialists there are in the field, the greater the chance for us as a group to make our voices heard and our influence felt, particularly in this era of budget cuts and job shuffling.

Fast Fact:

Read more about the number of NBCTs online at **http://www.nbpts.org/nbct/nbctdir_byyear.cfm**.

Table 7

Comparison of Current Library Media NBCTs by State

State	#of NBCTs as of 2004	Lib. Media NBCTs as of 2004
North Carolina	8280	278*
Florida	6364	200
California	3080	17
Ohio	2374	20
Georgia	1780	79

*North Carolina currently leads the nation in NBCTs in all certificate fields.

Explanation of the Five Core Propositions

Reforming the teaching force, then, must start with identifying the benchmarks for accomplished teaching and follow with a means for evaluating those who exemplify these benchmarks in their practice. The Five Core Propositions are the key factors that accomplished teachers should model regularly. Potential National Board candidates need to understand what each of these propositions means, both personally and professionally.

These Five Core Propositions are further defined by the National Board as follows:

Proposition #1, "teachers are committed to students and their learning," means that teachers "recognize individual difference in their students and adjust their practice accordingly, have an understanding of how students develop and learn, treat students equitably, and extend their mission beyond developing the cognitive capacity of their students." In other words, accomplished teachers and media specialists know that all children can learn. They recognize that students may learn

September 23

If I can become National Board certified, it should be a benefit not only to my own practice, but also to my school. Our school has been targeted in the local news media for being a "high priority" school under the No Child Left Behind Act. We made Adequate Yearly Progress last year, but we have to achieve AYP two years in a row to come off the "high priority" list. Now a few families want to transfer their kids out of our school. We are a good school! We have a wonderful staff—some of the best I've ever known. It seems like all we ever get is bad press, so maybe we need to turn that around. It should be a good thing to have a National Board Certified Media Specialist at our school! Maybe it will inspire others to seek certification, also.

differently and accommodate these different learning styles in their practice. They observe their students' interests and abilities and tailor their instruction accordingly. They also incorporate knowledge of how students grow and develop, and are aware of cultural differences and societal influences. They foster self-esteem in their students and motivate all and respect all, regardless of religious, racial, and cultural differences.

Proposition #2, "teachers know the subjects they teach and how to teach those subjects to students," means that "teachers appreciate how knowledge in their subjects is created, organized, and linked to other disciplines, command specialized knowledge of how to convey a subject to students, and generate multiple paths to knowledge." Another way of stating this is that teachers and media specialists have a deep understanding of the subjects they teach and how these subjects are integrated with other subject areas as well as real-life situations. Teachers and media specialists have an appreciation for the wisdom of the ages and uphold cultural literacy. In addition, accomplished teachers and media specialists know how to teach the principles of their subject matter while fostering critical and analytical thinking in their students. Accomplished teachers and media specialists know how to convey their subject matter to students. They modify their teaching as necessary to accommodate all learning styles and create multiple paths to knowledge.

Proposition #3, "teachers are responsible for managing and monitoring student learning," means "teachers call on multiple methods to meet their goals, orchestrate learning in group settings, place a premium on student engagement, regularly assess student progress, and are mindful of their principal objectives." In other words, teachers and media specialists are responsible for managing and monitoring student learning, so teachers and media specialists manage their classrooms so that students make effective use of their time. Accomplished teachers and media specialists strive for deep student engagement in all activities, and work with colleagues to complement their own teaching styles. Teachers and media specialists have a range of techniques for instruction and seek to eliminate ineffectual styles and routines that fail to motivate students. Teachers and media specialists maintain a disciplined environment and engage in multiple methods, including group discussion, peer coaching, face-to-face instruction and so on. Accomplished teachers engage in a variety of methods to assess the progress of their students and measure both individual student growth as well as the growth of the class as a whole. Teachers and media specialists can clearly convey student performance to the students themselves and their parents.

Proposition #4, "teachers think systematically about their practice and learn from experience," means "teachers are continually making difficult choices that test their judgment and seek the advice of others and draw on education research and scholarship to improve their practice." Accomplished teachers and media specialists, then, model the attributes they seek to foster in their students, and are willing not only to take risks, but also to adopt changes and experiment as necessary to determine the most effective methods to employ. Accomplished teachers and media specialists are lifelong learners who continually seek to grow and improve their practice. Moreover, accomplished teachers and media specialists critically examine the work they do and adapt their teaching strategies to new research findings and best practices of their profession.

Proposition #5, "teachers are members of learning communities," means that "teachers contribute to school effectiveness by collaborating with other professionals, work collaboratively with parents, and take advantage of community resources." In other words, accomplished teachers and media specialists are those who are willing to work collaboratively with other professionals in developing curriculum,

September 25

Today I made a chart of the Five Core Propositions and listed beside each one examples of how I meet these standards in my practice. I hope it will help me clarify my understanding of the standards and define what I already do that meets these benchmarks and what I need to do to align my practice with the standards. Gee, now that I reflect on the standards, I see that I really do know what accomplished practice is. And, the good thing is, I believe I am already doing things that could be considered accomplished.

defining policies and procedures, conducting staff development, and more. Teachers and media specialists are knowledgeable about the school and community resources that can benefit students and draw on those resources to enrich the instructional environment as needed. Accomplished teachers and media specialists find many ways to work collaboratively with parents for the betterment of their school.

Fast fact:

Read more about the Five Core Propositions online at **http://www.nbpts.org/about/coreprops.cfm**.

Table 8

The Five Core Propositions and Peggy's Practice

#1 "Teachers are committed to students and their learning."

I have a personal mission statement that reflects my commitment to my students; I have made school librarianship my lifelong career; I always seek to excel—to be the best teacher I can be and I challenge my students to set high goals for themselves, too! My mission is to model my love of literature and technology for my students and to introduce my students to a wide variety of resources so that they can not only learn to use them but also determine what resources best meet their needs and interests.

#2 "Teachers know the subjects they teach and how to teach those subjects to students."

I have studied ways to make information literacy accessible to even the youngest students and designed my own information literacy model especially for my students; I have been studying brain-based theories of instruction, as well as constructivist learning theories, and more. I want to reach all of my students in a way that is meaningful to them.

#3 "Teachers are responsible for managing and monitoring student learning."

Over the years, I have accumulated a "bag of tricks" for monitoring student behavior and have incorporated a variety of new assessment tools: rubrics, journals, group discussion, etc. I look at the lesson plans others have posted and collect best practices. I have designed multiple rubrics to use in my practice. I always try to look at test scores even though I don't teach all subject areas. It helps me to know where the school's weak areas are for collection development purposes.

#4 "Teachers think systematically about their practice and learn from experience."

I have incorporated daily reflection and journaling in my practice; I have amended my practice as needed to meet the needs of our ever-changing student population. I try to learn from my mistakes and seek advice from multiple sources often.

#5 "Teachers are members of learning communities."

I regularly read and post to the e-mail list and on school library distribution and discussion lists. I have started attending grade level meetings. I have conducted two share sessions for other media specialists in my district and attend as many as I can.

Chapter Three

THE NATIONAL BOARD LIBRARY MEDIA *Standards*

CHAPTER THREE AT A GLANCE

Journal Entry: October 1 40
Defining Accomplishment 41
Table 9: Defining the Accomplished Library Media Specialist 41
Journal Entry: October 2 42
Table 10: National Board Library Media Standards
and Peggy's Practice 44
Journal Entry: October 3 43
Table 11: Log of Community Interactions 46

October 1

It really helped me to write down examples from my own practice that align with the National Board's Five Core Propositions, so I plan to do the same thing with the National Board's ten standards for Library Media. I am thinking that this will help me as I start writing my portfolio entries, but I am not sure what I am going to write yet.

At any rate, writing out examples from my own practice will at least enlighten me on the weakest areas of my practice and perhaps make me feel accomplished in some areas! Right now, I believe I can document some significant accomplishments, but I am not sure how to show how they relate to student achievement. I know relating to student achievement is very important.

"The harder you work, the luckier you get."
—Gary Player

Defining Accomplishment

The last decade has ushered in dramatic changes to the responsibilities and workloads of school library media specialists. New technologies, online resources, automated circulation systems, and increasing amounts of patron data have stretched the duties of school library media specialists to near breaking points in some districts. At the same time, severe budget cuts, rising costs of print materials, increased demands for technology resources, and personnel cuts have added additional stress to the job. With all the changes in the profession, school library media specialists who simply do their jobs day to day are pretty remarkable. Those who "shine" while doing their jobs are truly exceptional. So, what practices signify "exceptionality" or "accomplishment" in the field? The answer is complex. An accomplished media specialist is one who has not only kept up with the changes in the field, but has been a change agent and a role model for peers, particularly with integrating technology, information literacy, literature appreciation, ethics and access, and so on. And most importantly, an accomplished media specialist, while exemplifying exceptional practice, also makes a significant contribution to student achievement.

Table 9

Defining the Accomplished Library Media Specialist

The accomplished library media specialist, then, is one who:

- *Exemplifies the five core propositions.*
- *Models the certificate area benchmarks identified by the National Board.*
- *Exceeds expectations.*
- *Increases student achievement.*
- *Presents solid evidence of best practices that are both concrete and measurable.*

Accomplishment in the field of library media represents exceptionality, high achievement, and exemplary practice. Accomplishment is not synonymous with competence. Practitioners who remain in their jobs each year are expected to be competent. Outstanding media specialists should be proud of their accomplishments and frank in documenting each one. Accomplishments that are submitted for Portfolio Entry #4, Documented Accomplishments, should directly relate to the ten National Board standards for Library Media and should directly correspond with student learning in the fields of information literacy, literature appreciation, reading achievement, ethical use of information resources, technology literacy, and any other related area of learning.

October 2

I have some ideas about ways my program exemplifies the five core propositions and the ten standards, but I am not clear how I can use these in my portfolio entries. Maybe some other people are wondering the same thing. I am going to start a discussion with members of my group about how they are going to incorporate the standards in their written entries. Maybe they will have a better understanding than I do!

In the meantime, I am going to list the ten library media standards and examples from my own practice to see how I might be able to incorporate these into my written portfolio entries. That should give me a starting point for discussion with my group.

October 3

I am taking the Knowledgeable Teacher course entirely online. I hope I don't miss out on any good discussion sessions this way, but the online presentation really suits my lifestyle right now. I think I might enjoy more classes online as this fits my lifestyle and I can work at my own pace and on my own schedule in accordance with the course expectations. I think I might investigate taking more online courses in my Ed.S. program at the university.

I am still monitoring the e-mail list for National Board candidates in library media and found a good tip: I am now keeping a log of all my interactions with community members. For example, I spoke with the owner of the local bookstore today. She wants to come by the school and talk about some storytelling events she is offering at her bookstore and see if we can coordinate an author visit at the school.

Also, I attended the PTA board meeting and offered to post any PTA announcements on the school news broadcast as well as update the school PTA Web page. I think these activities will constitute important interactions with the community but I am still not sure how to define community. Perhaps it means all the communities I can identify: the professional learning community within our school, the community of our school attendance area, the community within our cluster, our district, or our region.

National Board Library Media Standards and Peggy's Practice

#1 "Accomplished library media specialists have knowledge of learning styles and of human growth and development."

Since we have just added a pre-K class to our school, it is very important for me to be up on the latest theories of human growth and development, especially in early childhood. Also, we have a number of gifted students with learning differences. I serve all students in the school, so I am glad I took a course over the summer on educational psychology. I have just subscribed to some new educational journals and have joined the Association for Supervision and Curriculum Development and the International Society for Technology in Education as well.

#2 "Accomplished library media specialists know the principles of teaching and learning that contribute to an active learning environment."

Staying on top of changes in technology is demanding, but I am committed to it! I signed up to take a free training offered in my school district on creating distribution lists in our district e-mail and another on taking advantage of advanced features in our circulation system software. I value my technology expertise that allows me to work technology elements into nearly every lesson I teach for an active, resource-based learning activity. For example, when the third grade studied life cycles, I integrated a book with a student-created web in Inspiration and a PowerPoint four-slide show on the changes a tree experiences throughout the seasons.

#3 "Accomplished library media specialists know the principles of library and information studies needed to create effective, integrated library media programs."

I have noticed that the youngest students have a need to locate information, but don't know where to begin, so I designed my InfoQuest information literacy model to teach them principles of information literacy by actually researching an intriguing question related to the curriculum. When the fourth grade was studying states, the principal suggested a question related to state flags that drew in a record number of participants and generated a lot of interest in the program!

#4 "Accomplished library media specialists integrate information literacy through collaboration, planning, implementation, and assessment of learning."

I have worked closely with my administration to create a program unique to our school. "Compton Cubs are W.I.L.D." incorporates all four of the roles Loertscher (2000) defines in Taxonomies of the Library Media Program: collaboration, integration of technology, information literacy, and reading. I am presenting this program at the Summer Leadership Institute for administrators in my district.

#5 "Accomplished library media specialists lead in providing equitable access to and effective use of technologies and innovations."

My latest goal is to see that not only students but also teachers have access to the latest technology; I have been offering monthly trainings for both teachers and students on using the many resources we now have available, from laptops to video streaming, etc. so that technology is available to all users.

#6 "Accomplished library media specialists plan, develop, implement, manage, and evaluate library media programs to ensure that students and staff use ideas and information effectively."

I have planned, developed, implemented, and managed many good programs, but my weakest link in the past has been in evaluating programs for their effectiveness. I am now more committed to record keeping as I can see how it helps me promote my programs and gain support for them when I have visible evidence written down. It also helps me to adapt to the needs of my students by making improvements and adjustments as often as needed.

#7 "Accomplished library media specialists engage in reflective practice to increase their effectiveness."

I have started keeping a journal to reflect on my practice. It helps me not only to clarify my goals, but to see how I have grown and changed. This is the first real effort I have made at reflecting on my practice, but I can already see its value. Since I have to write reflectively in my portfolio entries, I am hoping this will help me strengthen that style of writing, as well.

#8 "Accomplished library media specialists model a strong commitment to lifelong learning and to their profession."

I am back in graduate school again, pursuing my Ed.S.—and I hope to eventually pursue my doctorate. If that is not a commitment to lifelong learning, I don't know what is.

#9 "Accomplished library media specialists uphold professional ethics and promote equity and diversity."

I have always been committed to professional ethics, but I am speaking up to all staff more often. I see so many violations, from teachers copying their home software onto their classroom workstations, to teachers and students downloading or copying and pasting files from the Internet. I am going to launch a campaign to educate everyone on ethics and legalities in the school setting. Teaching others should help me, too.

#10 "Accomplished library media specialists advocate for the library media program involving the greater community."

I have always valued parent volunteers, but I am beginning to see how important it is to have a "voice" with the PTA. I am always offering to help the PTA president and now I have been invited to attend a PTA board meeting. It is so important to have the support of the PTA in what I do, whether it is hosting a book fair, or asking for money for summer reading programs!

Fast fact:

Read more about the ten Library Media Standards online at http://www.nbpts.org/candidates/guide/04port/04_ecya_lm.html.

Table 11

Log of Community Interactions

Date	Event
10/1	Met with owner of local bookstore to discuss storytelling events that we could co-sponsor
10/1	Met with PTA president and offered to broadcast announcements and add to Web page
10/5	Shared ideas with other candidates on e-mail list
10/7	Presented research on National Board Certification to other media specialists in the district in a share session at my school
10/10	Submitted an article on National Board Certification to Library Media Connection magazine
10/15	Attended a district-wide inservice training on using district Web-based software to locate curriculum standards; used in collaborative planning with staff

Fast Fact:

Read more about advocating for your program within the greater community online at http://www.nbpts.org/events/products.cfm and http://www.nbpts.org/edreform/index.cfm.

Chapter Four

TIME MANAGEMENT AND ORGANIZATIONAL *Tips*

CHAPTER FOUR AT A GLANCE

Journal Entry: October 20	.48
Overview of the Process	.49
Journal Entry: October 25	.50
Average Time Commitment	.49
Organizing the Portfolio Instructions	.51
Journal Entry: October 28	.52
Table 12: Quick Tips for Organizing the Portfolio Instructions	.51
Strategic Planning	.51
Timesaving Tips	.51
Table 13: Schedule of Events for Certificate Completion	.53

October 20

The Knowledgeable Teacher course is helping me to internalize the vision of the National Board and what the certification process entails. Taking the course has forced me to familiarize myself with the ten standards for Library Media and evaluate my practice against those standards. It has helped me to consider my strengths and build on those to improve my program. It has also forced me to evaluate my weaknesses and seek to improve so that all components of my practice are solid.

I am beginning to see that the certification process is somewhat like completing a graduate degree. It requires work, study, research, and practice, and is time intensive. I need to adjust my other commitments so that I can focus on this process for the time being. This process is most valuable but is also very time consuming.

> *"The greatest waste in the world is the difference between what we are and what we could become."*
>
> —Dr. Ben Herbster

Overview of the Process

Beginning the National Board Certification process is somewhat like enrolling in a graduate degree program. Many National Board Certified Teachers admit that the amount of work required to attain certification is very time intensive, particularly the written portfolio entries. Completing each written entry is somewhat like completing a written graduate course project or writing a short graduate thesis. With four portfolio entries required, the labor involved in the process can be grueling.

Candidates can begin to get organized by getting a clear understanding of what the process entails and how they might complete it. Candidates should consider their finances and time to see if it is feasible at the present stage of their lives. Talking to other National Board Certified teachers about the process should help to form a clear picture of what commitments are required in terms of money, time, and effort.

Fast Fact:
Certified library media specialists in your area can be located through the National Board Web site at www.nbpts.org/nbct/nbctdir_byyear.cfm.

Average Time Commitment

Research indicates that the average candidate spends between 200 and 400 hours in portfolio development for National Boards, which factors out to about eight hours per week. Many candidates devote their weekends to getting portfolio work done, but those with families or a full social schedule may find that very difficult, particularly over the five months or more it takes to complete the certification process.

The best tactic is to divide up the work into small segments and then block off days on the calendar with no other commitments, so that the work can be stretched out, rather than crammed into an exhausting schedule. Allowing a sufficient amount of time for rewrites, proofreading, and mentor readings prevents stress and figures in time to fix mistakes and to start over when something isn't working well.

October 25

I hope I haven't underestimated the amount of time and work required to complete this, since I am starting relatively late in the school year. Maybe other candidates are feeling the same thing. I will check on the e-mail list and see if others started as late as I did and completed the process successfully.

At this time, I really don't know how I am going to get all of this work done! Now that I have started, the task seems almost overwhelming! I am worried that I have overcommitted myself. In order to live up to the task, I am going to have to discipline myself and stick to a tough schedule. I am going to block out days on the calendar and make myself work on my entries alone on those days. I think that is the only way I will finish the job.

Organizing the Portfolio Instructions

It is important to have a clear picture of what the portfolio entails before beginning the process in order to get organized. After reading through the requirements, candidates can divide the directions into folders for each section of the portfolio: general directions and introduction, Entry 1, Entry 2, Entry 3, Entry 4, forms, and general packing and shipping directions. Folders can be stored in a rolling storage bin or in movable crates. Three-ring binders are useful as they expand as the paper trail for each entry grows with the work in progress. Also, three-ring binders with pockets help to keep notes and references separated from the written entry. Color-coded folders and binders are useful for fast retrieval and easy organization of data while work is in progress. Once a portfolio is finished and ready to organize for shipping, the color-coding again is helpful in keeping the many pages orderly until they are ready to pack.

Fast Fact:

The portfolio for library media candidates can be obtained at http://www.nbpts.org/candidates/guide/04port/04_ecya_lm.html.

Table 12

Quick Tips for Organizing the Portfolio Instructions

Create a folder with instructions for each of the four portfolio entries and a separate folder for packing instructions.

Store the folders in a storage crate or rolling file cart.

Three-ring binders are helpful for storing tips for each entry with the folder of instructions.

Color-code all folders and binders for organizing and identifying work.

Fast fact:

Read more tips for organizing portfolio instructions online at www.cstp-wa.org/Accomplishedteaching/impact_studies/what_teachers_discovered_about_literacy_fullreport.pdf

Strategic Planning

As with any large task, the trick to conquering it is to have a plan of attack. A strategy that works is to:

1. *Plan all stages ahead of time, even if changes are made.*
2. *Organize time and paperwork.*
3. *Implement plans on or ahead of schedule.*
4. *Ask for help when needed.*

Timesaving Tips

Although National Board Certification is a high-stakes undertaking, it is not the time to reinvent the wheel. Use successful lessons from the past with improvements that reflect the library media standards and best practices. After all, you are trying to show that what you do every day represents accomplishment, right? You are not trying to change everything you do and hope that it makes a difference in student achievement. You need something effective, but tried and true.

October 28

Today I found a new organizational strategy: I can easily locate my portfolio work when I keep each portfolio entry in a color-coded hanging file folder. I have put all of the folders in a legal-sized rolling cart. As the paper trail on each entry grows, I can add another matching folder.

Keeping the work separated by color enables me to sort work at a glance, saving me time, especially when I only have an hour or so in the evenings to get some work done. As the folders grow, I plan to move my completed work to a three-ring binder and keep only current copies of work in the color-coded hanging folder.

It is best to focus on one portfolio entry at a time to avoid confusion and repetition. The following schedule is ideal for candidates who plan and prepare ahead of time.

Table 13

Schedule of Events for Certificate Completion

August
- Seek financing.
- Purchase supplies such as paper, printer ink, folders, etc. while back-to-school sales are underway.
- Download portfolio and evaluate candidacy requirements.
- Organize work space.

September
- Apply for candidacy.
- Gather permissions from parents, coworkers.
- Locate mentors and support groups.
- Read portfolio requirements carefully.
- Plan portfolio units.

October
- Begin documenting accomplishments.
- Write draft of Entry #4, Documented Accomplishments.
- At the end of the month, send entry to the proofreader for comments.
- Save comments in the folder with the work.

November
- Begin videotaping practice.
- Work with different people in creating videotapes.
- Create the two-minute pan of the media center for Entry #2.
- Videotape activity for Entry #2.

December
- Write draft of Entry #2, Appreciation of Literature.
- At the end of the month, send Entry #2 to the proofreader for comments.
- Save comments in the folder with the work.

January
- Videotape for Entry #3, Integrating Technology.
- Write draft of Entry #3.
- Send Entry #3 to the proofreader for comments.
- Save comments in the folder with the work.

February
- Collect student work samples for Entry #1, Collaboration.
- Write draft of Entry #1.
- Send Entry #1 to the proofreader for comments.
- Save comments in the folder with the work.

March
- Begin revising all entries, based on proofreader comments.
- Revise one entry per week.
- Submit portfolio.

April
- Register for Online Assessment to be in late May or June.
- Allow time to rest and recover.
- Begin study schedule, planning approximately one to two weeks to study for each of the six online assessment questions, depending on test date.

May or June
- Take online assessment.

July-October
- Rest and recover.
- Network with other candidates and NBCTs.
- Continue to grow professionally.
- Seek opportunities to advocate for National Board Certification.
- Mentor other candidates.
- Consider training to become a facilitator.
- Attend the National Board Conference.

November
- Watch for scores to be posted between the week before Thanksgiving and the end of December.

Chapter Five

OBTAINING Support

CHAPTER FIVE AT A GLANCE

Journal Entry: October 31	.56
Mentors	.57
Table 14: Peggy's List of Proofreaders	.57
State-Based Incentives	.57
Table 15: Financial Information for Candidates	.58
National Board Academies	.58
E-mail Lists	.58
Publications	.58
Table 16: Online Sources of Support for Candidates	.59
Applying for Candidacy	.59

October 31

Today I visited the National Board Web site (http://www.nbpts.org/events/products.cfm) to see what resources were available to help candidates. The National Board's Candidate Resource Center has a large number of online resources available such as videotapes, online video clips, links to brochures, articles, and other official publications, links to sources of financial support, and much more. At the Web site, I also learned about purchasing some materials from the National Board to help me prepare my portfolio entries. I think it will help me to look at videos of other National Board Certified Teachers so that I can understand the level of accomplishment required to become certified. Also, it may help me think of ideas for my own entries, once the time comes.

> *"Don't walk behind me, I may not lead.*
> *Don't walk in front of me, I may not follow.*
> *Just walk beside me and be my friend."*
>
> —Albert Camus

Mentors

While none of a candidate's portfolio entries should be written as if they were to be published, each one should still be grammatically correct, well organized, and written in clear and concise language. Entries should follow the portfolio guidelines exactly and meet all formatting requirements in order to be scored. Candidates may benefit from some initial writing practice and having proofreaders review their entries for clarity.

Table 14

Peggy's List of Proofreaders

Entry #1: Instructional Collaboration

Associate Professor at the University of Montana

Entry #2: Literature Appreciation

Associate Professor at the State University of West Georgia

Entry #3: Technology Integration

District Media Services Technology Integration Specialist

Entry #4: Documented Accomplishments

Gifted teacher in another school district

Alternative Readers:

Director of Media Services, Assistant Principal, Department Chair for Media and Instructional Technology, State DOE Media Services Coordinator

State-Based Incentives

Incentives for payment of candidate fees vary by state. States such as North Carolina pay the entire cost for candidates. In Georgia, once candidates complete The Knowledgeable Teacher course, the instructor sends a list of students who have completed the course to the state Professional Standards Commission. The Georgia Professional Standards Commission then issues a promissory note for $1,000 to candidates for partial fee payment. The remainder of the cost must come from candidates, but is reimbursable once certification is obtained. Some candidates seek grants and low-cost loans for fee payment. Companies such as Washington Mutual and State Farm offer grants to candidates.

Other companies may offer low-cost loans. Some school districts will pick up the cost. And local support often comes from PTA, Partners in Education, and local school funds. Benefits vary from state to state and are available on the National Board Web site.

> **Table 15**
>
> *Financial Information for Candidates*
>
> *Explanation of Fees and Their Deadlines*
> http://www.nbpts.org/candidates/guide/4_feecht.html
>
> *Scholarship Information*
> http://www.nbpts.org/candidates/availscholar.cfm
> http://www.nbpts.org/candidates/scholar.cfm
>
> *NEA Low-Interest Loans for Candidates*
> http://www.neamb.com/loans/loanbc.jsp
>
> *Individual State Incentives*
> http://www.nbpts.org/about/state.cfm

National Board Academies

In my area, specially trained National Board Certified Teachers host weekend academies for candidates. The academies offer help to candidates by reading portfolio entries, advising candidates on writing styles, offering time management tips, and more. The academies fill up quickly and are scheduled in advance. Usually a central location, such as a hotel, is the site for the weekend academies. Check your state teacher's association, state certification office, and other local resources for teachers to find information on these academies.

E-mail Lists

Candidate e-mail lists are a great tool for discussing thoughts, feelings, frustrations, and more with other candidates and sometimes, NBCTs. The lists are also a tool for locating tips and resources to help with your portfolios and online assessment questions. Yahoo groups (http://groups.yahoo.com/) is a great e-mail list just for library media candidates.

Publications

Many publications are available to provide general and specific information for candidates. The National Board offers a variety of publications, available on their Web site. Articles and videos are available for candidates to purchase at http://www.nbpts.org/events/products.cfm.

Table 16

Online Sources of Support for Candidates

Yahoo Groups E-mail List for National Board Candidates in Library Media
http://groups.yahoo.com/group/librarymedia/
http://www.geocities.com/educationplace/lmnbpts.htm

Graduate Credit for Candidates
http://aps.nbpts.org/ace/begin.cfm

Streaming Video Clips of NBCTs in Action
http://www.nbpts.org/highered/digitaledge.cfm

The Professional Standard Newsletter
http://www.nbpts.org/events/theprofessionalstandard.cfm

Accomplished Teacher Magazine Archives
http://www.nbpts.org/nbct/atmag.cfm

National Board Promotional Videos
http://www.nbpts.org/news/tv_news.cfm

Online News
http://www.nbpts.org/news/tv_news.cfm

Great Web Sites
http://www.geocities.com/educationplace/lmnbpts.htm
http://www.oklibs.org/~oaslms/resource_page.htm
www.nea.org/issues/certification/02guide.pdf
www.nea.org/issues/certification/writing.html
csmp.neop.edu/tcap/nbpts/tutorials/video.html

Fast Fact:

Read about the state by state incentives online at **http://www.nbpts.org/about/state.cfm**.

Applying for Candidacy

Candidates can apply online at www.nbpts.org. The application fee is $300 and can be paid online (the site is secure) with a credit card. Candidates can then check their profile (www.nbpts.org/myprofile?) to see if the payment has posted. The total cost for candidates is $2,300.

Chapter Six

PRODUCING QUALITY Videotapes

CHAPTER SIX AT A GLANCE

Journal Entry: November 2	.62
Videotaping Entries	.63
Table 17: General Videotape Requirements	.63
Producing Quality Videotapes	.63
Journal Entry: November 5	.64
Planning Portfolio Entries with Videotape Segments	.63
Journal Entry: November 10	.66
Journal Entry: November 15	.67
Seating Students for Videotaping	.65
Journal Entry: November 20	.68
Improving Lighting for Videotaping	.65
Improving Sound Quality for Videotaping	.65
Table 18: Videotaping Tips from the Pros	.69
Journal Entry: November 23	.70
Assessing Your Own Videotapes	.69
Table 19: Self-Scoring Rubric for Videotapes	.71

November 2

The first videotape I made for National Board was my two-minute pan of the media center, a requirement for Entry #2. Although it sounded very simple, I found this videotape to be very difficult to produce—much more difficult than I originally anticipated. First of all, I tried making the tape during the school day, but ran into lots of problems doing so. Either the bell rang, the intercom interrupted, or someone spoke: "Oh, sorry, is the camera on?" or, worse, people passed right in front of the camera, and I lost my train of thought. I finally gave up on the idea of producing a quality pan of the media center during the school day.

My best tactic was to come in over the weekend and tape when the media center was quiet and I would not be interrupted. It took me twelve tries to get one good two-minute clip.

Of course, I worried about the length. I finally wrote out the narration and timed myself, saying it over and over until I made it run about one minute and 50 seconds. That allowed for turning the camera on and off and for natural pauses while I was speaking or adjusting the camera.

When I actually taped the segment, I placed the camera on a dolly and set it in the center of the media center. Then, I rotated the camera around the room in a circle, pausing at various points to discuss my shelving arrangement or student work areas. I didn't actually move the camera from this location, but I did zoom in and out once or twice when I focused on something specific.

I learned from my mistakes on this one, but I would say that even though this was the shortest tape segment, it took me the most time to complete. I also learned that I need all the help I can get on videotaping, so I am going to see what resources are out there to help make good videotapes.

> *"All photos are accurate. None of them is the truth."*
> —Richard Avedon

Videotaping Entries

Videotaping your practice may be one of the trickiest portions of your portfolio, even for an experienced videographer. Before beginning your videotaping, make certain you are familiar with all the requirements of each videotape entry. Some of the videotape requirements are general to all segments.

> **Table 17**
>
> ### *General Videotape Requirements*
>
> *1. You must have signed permission slips from every staff member and student who is included on any videotape you submit.*
>
> *2. The National Board sets time limits on the tapes, as well. Know these in advance before you plan your lesson and begin to videotape. While your tapes may be shorter in length than what is allowed, you will not be scored on any portion that runs over.*
>
> *3. Finally, no editing is allowed. If you have a camera that inserts special effects into your tape, cut that feature off before taping. Once you cut on the camera, do not cut if off again until you have finished your tape segment. You may not combine segments, except in accordance with the portfolio requirements.*

Producing Quality Videotapes

In general terms, the better the quality of the equipment you use, the better the quality of your videotapes. Use the best camera, lighting, and sound equipment you can operate. Some candidates prefer to have someone else tape for them. While this might work for you, remember that you may need to tape multiple times before you are satisfied with your tape quality. It is also a good idea to tape several segments to see which one you think best represents your practice and the lesson you write up in your portfolio entry. While fire drills, intercom announcements, bells, and other interruptions are a regular part of the school day, they can adversely affect the quality of your tape as well as your lesson. Even the best class may have trouble getting back on task after a fire drill.

Planning Portfolio Entries with Videotape Segments

Portfolio Entries 2 and 3 require videotapes, so these entries, in particular, should have an adequate time frame for making retakes and rewrites. Videotaping alone may take multiple attempts before a quality tape is created. Also, as candidates begin videotaping, the written analysis and reflection portions of the written entry may change as candidates comment on the contents of the videotape they submit with an entry.

November 5

I can't believe it! I set up with the gifted teacher to film her students in a lesson and wouldn't you know it—the network installers who were supposed to show up the day before were late arriving and came just when I had set up to videotape. I asked the installers how long it would take them to install the network drop and conduit. They promised to be finished in one hour, so I rescheduled my class for an hour-and-a-half later in the day. Of course, the installers weren't done on time! We postponed again as long as we could and then started taping anyway. To my total horror, while I was filming, the installers not only dropped the pipe with a loud bang, but were also hammering and shouting in the background. I am amazed that the students stayed focused on the lesson because it was nearly impossible for me to focus!

If you are not setting up the camera yourself, carefully choose a coworker to videotape for you. Make sure your coworker understands the requirements of the video: the tape must be continuous—no stopping and restarting or editing during the segment.

Videotapes may take several tries to perfect, so it is best to plan an extended lesson that you can tape over several days' time. That way, you can select the best segment to submit with your written portfolio entry, without having to start over on your plans.

Fast Fact:
A videotape guide produced for National Board candidates, NBPTS Video Production 101 Tutorial, from the California Arts Project, is available at **csmp.ucop.edu/tcap/nbpts/tutorials/video.html**.

Seating Students for Videotaping

Seating the students is important to the quality of tape you create. First of all, their faces should be seen in order for the assessor to hear their comments, note their interaction in the lesson, and see their expressions. Rather than aiming the camera in a straight line facing you, you should place the camera at an angle so that your face and the faces of your students can be seen at the same time. One arrangement that works well is to place the camera to the side of the room and set it for a wide-angle zoom so that while you are facing the students, your face and their faces can be seen at the same time. Another arrangement is to stand behind the students and put the camera at the front of the room. Then, as you move around the room, working with students, your face and theirs can be seen. Also, having a skilled cameraperson manning the camera for you might be an option so that panning and zooming is handled well.

Improving Lighting for Videotaping

Lighting is of critical importance in making a good quality tape. Darker skin tones may not show up well against a light background as the light background reflects light and "fools" a camera into accepting the available lighting as adequate. If you can choose a darker background such as a stained bookshelf or dark bulletin board, the camera will compensate by adding extra light to the subjects. Background lighting may also be desirable to better reflect the darker skin tones. If background lighting is available, by all means, take advantage of it, but make certain the bright lights themselves are not visible in the videotape. They should merely reflect on the subjects. Always tape and play back a test tape before beginning the actual taping you hope to use for your portfolio entry.

Improving Sound Quality for Videotaping

Sound is crucial to the quality of the tape. Most video cameras have a built-in microphone but this feature may not be adequate for good sound quality on your videotape entries. A quality tape should play back without having to increase the volume setting on the television and videocassette player in order to hear the subjects. Raising the volume setting during playback might increase the amount of white noise in the background and thus reduce the audio quality overall. It is important for assessors to not only hear what the candidates in the tape have to say, but also to hear what the students have to say.

If possible, obtain a microphone to enhance the sound quality. A wireless microphone can be passed to each student without getting any wires tangled. An omni-directional tabletop microphone is another good option. Placed in a central location, it can enhance sound quality without being moved to individual

November 10

During my initial attempt to videotape one entry, I was dismayed to learn that my coworker not only started and stopped the tape throughout but also spoke to students while behind the camera. Of course the tape was not usable and I had to start over with a different lesson at another time.

November 15

I found that making a videotape of my practice, a task that normally seems so routine, is much more difficult than I realized. First of all, not all of my students returned their permission slips to be videotaped. Since I am having to work with two different classes to obtain permission slips, it is up to the teacher to get these letters sent home and returned. Close collaboration allowed me to check regularly to find out the status of the forms. But one student was living in special circumstances and her mother refused to sign the form. I had to seat her under the camera so that she would not appear in any of the videos. Seating the students for the best quality tape was a task in itself.

November 20

I can't believe I didn't think about the white background working well with the fourth grade I am using for Entry 2. I made a tape of a lesson that I thought turned out so perfectly that I wouldn't change anything in it, only to find that I couldn't use the tape after all. Against the white background, the dark skin tones of some of the kids didn't show up at all! I knew to ensure I had good lighting before I started taping. I even checked with the custodian to have some bulbs replaced last week.

I was so disappointed about this. Not checking the background ahead of time is one mistake I will be sure not to repeat. I will make sure I have a dark background and bright lights for all my tapes after this. I never knew how important lighting was to the quality of my tapes before, but I can personally testify to it now. I will be sure to tell my group so others can learn from my experience.

students as they speak. Vendors such as Radio Shack sell these at a reasonable price (approximately $50). These microphones must be connected to speakers or an amp and speakers. Place the speakers close to the camera for best sound reproduction going into the video. If the camera has an external microphone jack, feed the microphone directly into the camera.

> **Table 18**
>
> ## *Videotaping Tips from the Pros*
>
> - *Use the fastest tape speed; slowing down will reduce the quality of your tape.*
> - *Use the best formats available; Super VHS is considered better quality than VHS.*
> - *Use high quality or professional equipment.*
> - *Light your area. Turn on any available light. Existing light may not be sufficient to show facial expressions, especially for darker skin tones, and reduces the quality of your recording. Aim at darker backgrounds whenever possible to avoid reflecting light into the camera.*
> - *Add a microphone and speakers. All video camcorders have a built-in microphone. However, the sound quality may be poor, especially since classrooms are generally not acoustically well built. Background noise can disrupt the sound quality. And, a built-in microphone may not be powerful enough to pick up all voices clearly. If you can add a microphone, do so. If the camera is not equipped for an external microphone, hook up to an amp, and speakers. Set the speakers near the camera so the sound will be amplified going in.*
> - *Add "dead" space before and after you tape. This makes for easier copying of your tape when the time comes.*
> - *Try to make only one copy—quality is lost with each generation of copying. When you copy, use the highest quality connections—S-video is preferable to composite (RCA) cables. It is not necessary to buy and use the gold-plated connectors, but don't settle for cheap cables, either. Use a dual-head video copier, or pay to have your videos copied by a professional. And speaking of copies, you will need to keep one for a backup in case yours is lost or damaged in the mail.*
> - *Practice makes perfect. Don't expect your videos to be made the first time around. Allow plenty of time to perfect the videos and choose the best ones to submit.*
> - *Terry McConnell and H.W. Sprouse have published a videotape guide especially for media specialists: Video Production for School Library Media Specialists: Communication and Production Techniques, available from Linworth Publishing. In addition, Keith Kyker and Christopher Curchy have a number of books on videotape production for school news shows and give tips on working with typical school-type equipment. Their Educator's Survival Guide for Television Production and Activities (2003) is recommended.*

Fast Fact:

A free videotape guide is available online at *http://www.focusinfo.com/support/articles/vedit.html*.

Assessing Your Own Videotapes

Now that you have made some videotapes, how would you assess them? Try viewing each tape as an assessor might and score yourself. You can use a rubric, if you like, to make it seem more authentic.

November 23

Today I actually made a good videotape. I think it is finally one I can use. I am going to try to watch it in a different light—guessing what an assessor might be looking for in the tape. I think if I can view it with a critical eye, I can see if it will do for my portfolio entry. I have read all the tips on the e-mail list. I read the portfolio instructions several times. I think I know what I should include, but I also know how difficult it is to make a perfect tape. Surely assessors don't expect perfection, do they?

I already know the sound and lighting should be good. I also know it is important to show interaction with the students. I wonder what else an assessor might be trying to see in the tape? I am going to ask my group what they think on this.

First, consider the environment of your media center or the classroom where you instruct students with your lesson. What is visible in the background? What displays can be seen? Is student work a focal point? Is the room inviting to your students? What sort of furniture arrangement is visible?

Next, consider the interactions you have with your students. Do you have whole group instruction? Small group instruction? One-on-one tutoring? Can student comments be heard? Who else is speaking and why? Are students speaking to you? Are students speaking to each other?

Finally, consider how engaged the students are. Are they responding to you? Are they responding to each other? Are they effectively following through with the assignment you have made? What indicators are visible on the tape of how the students feel about the activity?

Overall, how would you score yourself? What evidence can you see to support your score? Can you see student facial expressions? Can you clearly hear your instruction to a whole group? Can you clearly hear student responses? Do you play more than one role in instruction—in other words, if you start as the "sage on the stage," do you remain there, or do you also star as the "guide on the side?" Are there any "teachable moments" evident in the videotape? Is the evidence "clear, consistent and convincing?" or could you improve on your tape?

Table 19

Self-Scoring Rubric for Videotapes

	Consistently Evident in Tape	Clearly Evident in Tape	Evident on a Limited Basis in Tape	Little or No Evidence in Tape
Evidence of bright and inviting environment				
Evidence of multiple modes of instruction throughout tape				
Evidence of student engagement and on-task behaviors throughout tape				
Evidence of student interaction with the instructor and each other throughout tape				
Evidence of impact on student achievement as a result of instruction strategies used throughout the tape				
Quality of lighting, sound and instruction on tape overall				

Chapter Seven

SCORING RUBRICS AND Assessment Tips

CHAPTER SEVEN AT A GLANCE

Journal Entry: December 15 74
Overview of the Scoring Process 75
What Matters in Scoring 75
Journal Entry: December 20 76
Who Are the Assessors? 77
Table 20: Qualifications for Becoming an Assessor 77
Assessor Training 79
Table 21: Training Sessions for Assessors 79
Incentives for National Board Assessors 79
Journal Entry: December 30 78
Scoring Rubrics 79
How to Estimate Your Scores 80
Assessment Tips 81

73

December 15

I am making progress on all of my portfolio entries, but I am not sure if what I am writing for my entries truly identifies accomplishment in my field. I have carefully read the portfolio directions and followed them, but I want to know more about how my entries will be scored and what counts in scoring. This is important to know now so that I don't waste time on things that are unimportant or unrelated to the best scores. I don't have time to spend rewriting much as I am on a tight schedule now—writing one portfolio entry per month. What I write has to be quality material the first time around.

Moreover, I think I am accomplished, but how do I convey that to the assessors? How do I make every part of my entries count toward the highest scores? Of course I want to do well, so what exactly comprises the highest scores?

All of these questions are running through my mind and I am dedicated to finding the answers. I will discuss this with my support group and see what they think. In the meantime, I am going to read through the scoring guide very carefully. I know I can't hope to comprehend everything the first time around, so I plan to read it more than once and refer to it often while I work.

> *"You have to be first, different, or great.*
> *If you're one of them, you may make it."*
>
> —Loretta Lynn

Overview of the Scoring Process

The National Board scoring process is carefully monitored to be of highest integrity. The Educational Testing Service supervises the production of National Board assessment materials while Harcourt Educational Measurement prints and distributes the materials and processes candidate applications and submissions. Both the Educational Testing Service and Harcourt Educational Measurement share the responsibility of monitoring the scoring process.

Assessors in each certificate field are solicited from certified practitioners in that field. Library Media assessors, for example, are practicing library media specialists, some of whom may be National Board certified themselves, so they know how grueling the process is for candidates. Assessors are screened and must complete a rigorous training session after which they may or may not be hired to assess. During the actual scoring, assessors are closely monitored to ensure they score objectively and consistently.

All scores are based on a four-point rubric. Candidates who meet or exceed the expectations for a particular entry score 3s and 4s. Candidates who do not meet expectations for a particular entry score 1s and 2s. To score a 4, a candidate must demonstrate "clear, consistent, and convincing evidence" of having met the expectations for that entry. A score of 3 is "clear" evidence. A score of 2 indicates "limited" evidence, while a 1 indicates "little or no" evidence of having met the expectations for that entry. It is possible for a candidate to score low on one section and still achieve certification, if the other scores are high enough. Portfolio scores are obviously the most important, particularly for Entries 1 to 3. High scores in these three entries are a must. The online assessment is important but counts less toward the overall total. Scores for each entry are weighted and totaled to determine a final score. Certificates are awarded to candidates who achieve a total of 275 points or more. The portfolio entries are weighted at 16%, 16%, 16% and 12%, respectively. Online assessment questions are weighted at 6.67% each. Candidates can expect to see their scores posted online sometime between the week before Thanksgiving and the end of December.

What Matters in Scoring

Specific qualities of entries are valued in the scoring process. For example, each candidate's responses are scrutinized for adherence to the library media standards and the five core propositions, for carefully following instructions provided, and for specific details supplied.

December 20

It seems like last summer was a long time ago. I knew so little about the National Board when I applied to be an assessor. I was delighted to be accepted. I know the training was intense and that I worked diligently as an assessor and carefully fulfilled all that I was hired to do. I came out of the scoring process feeling confident that it was of highest integrity and that all of the scoring was appropriate. I had great respect for the entire process after having been a part of it.

But now that I am a candidate, I am wondering who the next round of library media assessors will be. Will they score my work fairly? How can I be confident that they will understand how much of my heart and soul has gone into this process? Will my entries represent my best work? I am so full of questions about how my work will be scored. I need to feel confident that I can best represent myself and that all the evidence I am sending will be sufficient to earn certification. It seems so different on the opposite side of the fence.

Assessors are trained to be thoroughly knowledgeable of the standards related to the entry being scored and for the specific instructions given for that entry. Candidate responses are scored with a four-point rubric. Assessors evaluate the candidate's response using a note-taking guide and consider the evidence against benchmarks representing the four levels of the rubric. Assessors score the entry using an Exercise Scoring Record to report and organize specific evidence found in that candidate's entry. Then the total entry is analyzed in relation to the benchmarks and scored accordingly. Candidates are not scored in comparison to each other, but in comparison to the benchmarks and standards which define accomplished teaching in the field of library media.

The National Board scoring process is standards-based rather than norm-referenced. This means that there is a standard of performance that candidates must meet in order to achieve certification. The standards for library media were developed by practicing library media specialists and accomplished teachers from many regions and ethnically diverse areas. Their work was carefully reviewed by the National Board for Professional Teaching Standards and then was field-tested in draft form all over the United States before being accepted as final. These standards define the rigorous and appropriate goals of accomplished practice in the field of library media and are the basis for the portfolio exercises, the online assessment questions, and the rubrics by which these are scored.

Fast fact:
Scoring guides are available online at http://www.nbpts.org/candidates/scoringguides.cfm.

Who Are the Assessors?

Assessors are selected from a pool of applicants who are currently practicing library media specialists. Assessors must have a valid teaching certificate and show proof of current employment in the field in which they are applying to assess. Like candidates, they must have taught in the field they assess for at least three years. Assessors go through a rigorous training period in order to be selected to assess.

Table 20

Qualifications for Becoming an Assessor

To become a National Board Assessor, candidates must:

- *Have a baccalaureate degree from an accredited institution.*
- *Have a valid teaching certificate, if required by the school.*
- *Have completed a minimum of three years of teaching in a pre-K to12 school.*
- *Be employed in at least half-time teaching position in the certificate area for which he or she is applying to assess or be a National Board Certified Teacher (NBCT) in that certificate area.*
- *Not currently be a candidate or nonachieving candidate for National Board Certification.*
- *Successfully complete National Board assessor training.*

Fast fact:
Read more about requirements for becoming an assessor at http://www.nbpts.org/standards/assessors.cfm.

December 30

I keep reading about "evidence" so I know this is a key word that I must focus on. My previous experience with evidence has always been related to a courtroom, but I think this may work as an analogy for me. If I consider my candidacy as a trial to prove that I am indeed an accomplished teacher, then my jury will be composed of my peers and each of my portfolio entries can become an exhibit in the trial. I know that there are many ways a library media specialist can be considered accomplished and there are many accomplished library media specialists who are practicing nationwide. My case for certification will depend on how strong the evidence I present is in support of my case. Each exhibit I submit is another testimony to my accomplishment, but is it evidence that is convincing enough to win over a jury of my peers?

Assessor Training

Trained assessors must be able to evaluate candidate entries on the basis of the standards alone while ignoring their own personal preferences and biases. Not every assessor applicant is capable of withholding their biases and relying solely on the standards to recognize accomplished practice. During training, applicants for scoring carefully review instructions for a particular entry or exercise which they are assigned to score. They also focus on the standards and the scoring criteria as well as the benchmarks and rubric. Assessors will have a period of scoring where they score just for practice. Their scoring responses will be evaluated against expert assessments. The trainer will then lead a discussion on how the experts scored the entries and how the trainees scored in comparison. Only the trainees whose accuracy and quality of scores meet assessment standards are invited to score actual candidate performances. All scoring is carefully monitored throughout the entire scoring process.

> **Table 21**
>
> ### Training Sessions for Assessors
>
> Sessions cover:
> - *An orientation to the National Board certification process.*
> - *The National Board Five Core Propositions, the National Board Library Media Standards, and the Library Media candidate instructions.*
> - *An explanation of the scoring system, the scoring scale, the rubrics, benchmarks, Exercise Scoring Record, and other scoring tools.*
> - *Extensive training on biases and preferences, including self-examination and awareness of both.*
> - *Individual and group analyses of sample candidate performances.*
> - *Demonstration of an ability to successfully score sample candidate performances.*

Scoring sessions are carefully monitored and conducted at specifically designated scoring sites. Assessors generally work from 8:30 a.m. until 5 p.m. with lunch and snacks provided on site. Assessors do not leave the site during the day and all scoring is confidential. Assessors generally live close to the assessment site but some may travel to the site for the scoring sessions. Sessions generally last up to two weeks, depending on the number of candidates and the number of assessors available to score at a session. Assessors are paid and may earn additional incentives for scoring.

Incentives for National Board Assessors

- *Graduate credit hours.*
- *$125 per day honorarium for each full day scoring.*
- *Special offers for future candidacy for assessors serving at least two years.*
- *Professional development opportunities.*

Scoring Rubrics

Because the goal of accomplished teaching is to set high and appropriate standards for student learning, every candidate entry must reflect a strong and obvious connection between the activity and student achievement. All of the scoring is based exclusively on candidate evidence submitted. Implied evidence is not scored and missing evidence is not acknowledged. Assessors do not make comments on the entries but simply evaluate the evidence presented.

The highest level of the rubric, 4, is characterized by "clear, consistent, and convincing evidence." The evidence for each entry varies, depending on the entry and the instructions given, but candidates should follow all instructions carefully and completely. A level 4 response generally indicates that a candidate displays a thorough knowledge of the standards, consistently utilizes appropriate instructional practices, employs a variety of techniques, and demonstrates detailed description, in-depth analysis, and insightful reflection into what worked well and what should be improved in the future.

The next level, 3, is characterized by "clear" evidence that a candidate displays knowledge of the standards, utilizes appropriate instructional practices, employs multiple learning strategies, and demonstrates detailed description, in-depth analysis, and insightful reflection into what worked well and what should be improved in the future. Both a level 3 and a level 4 are considered accomplished scores. The difference in a level 3 and a level 4 score is in the consistency. One part of the level 3 response may be more detailed and thorough than another, but taken as a whole, the level 3 response clearly indicates evidence of accomplishment.

The next level, 2, is characterized by "limited" evidence. The response shows unconvincing evidence that a candidate has a thorough knowledge of the standards, utilizes appropriate instructional practices, employs a variety of teaching strategies, and demonstrates limited description, analysis that lacks depth, and reflection that may be loosely or unconnected to the instructional sequence. Some parts of the response may be effective, but the response overall may be inappropriate, weak, sketchy, or vague.

The final level, 1, is characterized by "little or no" evidence. This response may be erroneous, incomplete, unrelated, or simply ineffective. Both level 2 and level 1 are considered to be less than accomplished. Candidates with these scores on a portfolio entry or assessment center exercise may need additional work in these areas if the total score is less than 275.

How to Estimate Your Scores

The scores for each entry are weighted so that you can anticipate how you might score based on the areas where you feel you have strengths. For example, the first three portfolio entries count the most and are most heavily weighted of all the scores. The assessment center exercises are weighted equally. Therefore, you can assume that the first three portfolio entries are the ones for which you need to score the highest and the assessment center exercises all carry an equal chance of increasing (or decreasing) your total score. Let's assume, then, that you anticipate scoring a 3 on the first two portfolio entries, but you feel that you may have scored a bit lower on the portfolio entry three because technology is not your strongest area. This may affect your score on the technology question in the assessment center exercise, as well, but you feel that you may have compensated for it with your strength in information literacy. With this knowledge, you can predict what you think your final total might be. The first two portfolio entries are weighted at 16%, so a score of 3 x 16 will give you a weighted score of 48 on these two entries. A score of 2 on the third entry x 16 will give you a weighted score of 32. The fourth portfolio entry is weighted at 12%, so assuming you scored at least a 3, you can estimate a weighted score of 36. The subtotal for the portfolio, then, would be 48 + 48 + 32 + 36 = 164.

Now, assuming that you scored a 3 on the first two assessment center exercises, your weighted score for these items would be 3 x 6.67%, or 20.01 each. The third item, on technologies, might be scored a 2, so the weighted score for this item would be 2 x 6.67%, or 13.34. Suppose that you scored a 3 on item number 5, information literacy, but only scored a 2 on items 4 and 6. Your weighted scores would then be 3 x 6.67, or 20.01, and 2 x 6.67, or 13.34, and 2 x 6.67, or 13.34. Your total for the assessment center items, then, would be 20.01 + 20.01 + 13.34 + 20.01 + 13.34 + 13.34 = 100.05. All candidates have a uniform constant of 12 added to their total weighted scores, so your total weighted score, then, would be 164 + 100.05 + 12 = 276.05, a passing score. This score, however, does not allow any room for overestimating or misjudging the amount of detail or significance of a particular item in the instructions.

Remember, this exercise is only an estimate and cannot be considered accurate. The purpose of this estimation is to help a candidate consider areas where extra work might be needed. Candidates should not assume that they are qualified to score based on knowledge of the rubric and the standards alone. A lot of training goes into preparing assessors to score fairly and in accordance with the rubrics, the standards, and the established benchmarks for each entry.

Assessment Tips

While candidates cannot fake knowledge they do not have, they can increase the odds of their success by following a few simple guidelines in their submissions.

- *The easiest way to do your best on each entry is to read and understand what you are being asked to do.*
- *Do not skip any part of the instructions or overlook any of the questions or prompts in your response.*
- *Give detailed descriptions whenever possible and avoid vague or sketchy comments.*
- *In your analysis, relate your responses to the standards to show insight into what is considered accomplishment in the practice of library media.*
- *Show a clear and convincing link to student achievement whenever possible.*
- *Check for grammatical and spelling errors, and write in clear prose.*
- *Avoid wordiness, professional jargon, acronyms, and abbreviations.*
- *Back up your statements, whenever possible, with specific examples from your own practice.*
- *Avoid incomplete ideas, erroneous comments, vague details, and ideas that are not clearly related to best practices in the field and cannot be supported with research.*

Chapter Eight

PORTFOLIO WRITING *Styles*

CHAPTER EIGHT AT A GLANCE

Journal Entry: January 1 84
Portfolio Entries for the Library Media Certificate Field 85
Journal Entry: January 5 86
National Board Writing Styles 85
Analytical Writing 87
Tips for Better Analytical Writing 87
Descriptive Writing 87
Tips for Better Descriptive Writing 87
Reflective Writing 89
Tips for Better Reflective Writing 88
Journal Entry: January 7 89
Table 22: Portfolio Writing Styles 89
Table 23: Tips for Improving Written Entries 90

83

January 1

Today I visited the www.nbpts.org Web site and downloaded the library media portfolio. It is over 250 pages! I decided to print a few pages at a time since my old printer doesn't have much memory. But printing this way also allows me to read each section thoroughly so that I have an understanding of what that portion of the portfolio entails. I am putting each segment into a three-ring binder and keeping notes of my thoughts in the margin as I read.

> *"The man who moves a mountain begins by carrying away small stones."*
>
> —Confucius

Fast Fact:
Library Media Portfolio instructions are available online at
http://www.nbpts.org/candidates/guide/04port/04_ecya_lm.html.

Portfolio Entries for the Library Media Certificate Field

The portfolio is a multifaceted snapshot of a candidate's practice. It provides written details about the school and students in it, analysis of student work, reflection on practices that worked and didn't work. Student work samples, videotapes, and documents of professional growth, teacher leadership, and community interaction round out the picture.

Fast Fact:
See samples of exemplary teaching units at *http://ali.apple.com/ali_sites/deli/*.

Candidates for National Board Certification in Library Media are required to submit four portfolio entries: Instructional Collaboration, Literature Appreciation, Integration of Instructional Technologies, and Documented Accomplishments. In addition to written commentary, Entry 1 requires student work samples, Entries 2 and 3 require videotapes, and Entry 4 requires documentation such as award certificates, degrees, letters from parents, and other examples of exemplary practice. Written portfolio entries require three different writing styles throughout: descriptive, analytical, and reflective.

National Board Writing Styles

Three different writing styles are required for each portfolio entry—descriptive, analytical, and reflective. Descriptive portions of an entry should explain the setting, the students, and the subject matter. Analytical portions of a portfolio entry should explain the rationale for the procedures followed and the expected outcomes. Reflective portions on an entry should discuss whether goals were met or not and what changes might be made in the future to better meet the needs of students or better instruct them in areas where they may have fallen short of the goals for the lesson.

January 5

My instructor for the Knowledgeable Teacher course advised me to write some sample entries for the portfolio. While these won't be the ones I submit once I officially apply for certification, they will help her to evaluate my writing styles and see if they meet criteria for my certificate field. Also, writing sample entries will help me to become accustomed to the different writing styles that are required for each entry and begin to focus my thoughts on each entries requirements. I already know that descriptive writing requires attention to specific details about my teaching situation, my students, and my school. I also know that analytical writing is where I explain why and how I am carrying out an instructional sequence with my students. I am not used to writing reflectively, though. I tend to do this mentally without thinking about it, as I go through each day. I may stop an activity in midstream when I realize what is not working with my students and take a different approach. I don't have a lot of experience writing about this sort of reflection, though.

Analytical Writing

Analytical writing defines the reason for the structure, content, and pacing of a particular lesson with a particular group of students and generally answers the questions "What?" and "Why?" An example of analytical writing might be: "Because the first grade social studies standards in our district require students to identify the elements of a community, and because the district technology standards require students to be able to use a mouse and drawing tools, to open, save, and close a file and to print, the classroom teacher and I collaborated on a lesson where the students each drew an imaginary community using the software program, Inspiration. Students included schools, service providers such as hospitals and fire stations, governmental buildings such as courthouses and jails, and residential areas and commercial areas in their communities. Students were also required to name their community and include a key. The students saved their work to a floppy disk and printed out their finished projects in color."

Tips for Better Analytical Writing

- *Avoid too much description.*
- *Seek to interpret student responses.*
- *Ask yourself "Why?" and "How do you know?" and provide explicit answers.*
- *Prescribe goals for improvement.*

Descriptive Writing

Descriptive writing may be mixed with analytical writing throughout the entry. Descriptive writing usually answers the questions "Who?" and "Where?" and details the ages, abilities and interests of the students in the class while commenting on any unusual circumstances that are characteristic of the class. For example, one descriptive entry might read, "The class consists of 30 second grade students with a wide range of ability levels. While the number of boys and girls is fairly even, 14 boys and 16 girls, a large number of students speak English as a second language (37%), and an even greater number of students come from single-parent homes (58%). The majority of students (69%) are on a free and reduced lunch plan, and most eat breakfast at school as well. Over 50% of the students remain after dismissal in the After School Program. While 9 students receive academic assistance in the Early Intervention Program, only 1 student participates in the Gifted Program."

Tips for Better Descriptive Writing

- *Note significant details such as socioeconomic factors, class size, transience that may affect student achievement.*
- *Include details that make a difference in your situation such as having a blind or physically handicapped student.*
- *Note unique traits of students such as tendency to write better after having created a drawing for their story, or to focus better once they have physically moved through the steps for practice.*

January 7

I am having a hard time writing reflectively. While I know that I reflect on the things I do with my students, I find it hard to put these thoughts into words. One thing that I have decided to do to improve my reflection is to keep a journal. I am not going to stick to any particular writing style, but just get in the habit of putting my thoughts down on paper as I go through National Board certification. As I go back to write up reflective statements on each portfolio entry, I can look over the things I have written in my journal. Perhaps getting my thoughts down on a regular basis will help strengthen my ability to reflect on my practice.

I wonder if other people feel the same way I do about reflection? I am going to ask my support group about this.

Reflective Writing

Reflection generally falls at the end of the entry and incorporates the material from the earlier sections into a summary. Reflection can include statements indicating satisfaction with the progress students made or the hope of improving a segment of the lesson in the future. For example, a reflective comment might read, "All students completed their projects on time and with a minimum of intervention to keep them on track. Most students were proud of their accomplishments and eager to show off their work on Parent Night. While the project met the goals established for student achievement, in the future, I would like to see more parental involvement in the project and greater turnout for the student presentations at Parent Night. In order to draw more parents in, I would like to invite parents to become actively involved as hosts or hostesses for the evening or to take an active role in greeting, decorating, setting up, or cleaning up. With a specific job to fulfill, I hope that more parents will be in attendance for this important event to create an audience for students to showcase their hard work."

Reflection is a powerful opportunity for a candidate to give evidence of professional growth. Just as no one is a perfect teacher, no candidate should expect her portfolio entries to give evidence of a perfect instructional sequence or activity. In describing what worked and what didn't work well within an instructional sequence, a candidate can define weak areas that can be improved and set goals for the future to implement the growth needed for improvement. Reflection can and should incorporate a plan for collaboration with other teachers who demonstrate strengths in a candidate's weak areas, reading professional publications in the areas of needed growth, seeking input from instructional lead teachers and administrators, and taking staff development or graduate courses in target areas.

Tips for Better Reflective Writing

- Explain whether or not learning goals were met.
- Explain any student misconceptions.
- Think of possible ways that this activity might be improved to further student understanding of the concepts.
- What worked with this type of lesson before?
- What feedback did you receive from your students?
- How will you use the information you gained from this experience?

Table 22

Portfolio Writing Styles

Descriptive *writing provides the setting for the instruction (who, when, where), reveals knowledge, and details goals, procedures, and the objectives for a specific lesson.*

Analytical *writing provides insight into the planning and rationale behind a lesson and provides evidence of accomplishment, interprets the evidence, and explains (what, why).*

Reflective *writing reviews the evidence, draws conclusions, and considers where change or improvement is needed in the future (how can I improve?).*

Fast Fact:

Learn more about NBPTS writing styles online at
http://www.coe.ilstu.edu/ilnbpts/Candidates/PortfolioResources.asp#Writing_for_Your_NBPTS_Portfolio.

Table 23

Tips for Improving Written Entries

- *Candidates should read the directions for each entry and follow them very closely, including formatting, responding to prompts, and otherwise meeting criteria. When preparing a written entry, candidates should seek to keep responses to the point and "meaty." Fluff and fillers have no place in the written response—every word counts!*

- *Candidates may find it helpful to have another person read their entries—someone who can be objective and read with a critical eye to help a candidate identify areas of weakness in the written document. Of course, calling on other candidates in the same certificate field would not be advisable, but many National Board Certified Teachers are available to mentor new candidates. To find National Board Certified Teachers in your area, visit http://www.nbpts.org/nbct/for.cfm.*

- *Some candidates have met with success by copying and pasting the directions for each portfolio entry in bold type into a formatted word processing document and leaving a space for their written response. Once the response is entered, the candidate can quickly look back at the directions to determine if all parts have been addressed. Once the entry writing is complete, the boldface directions can be deleted.*

- *Keeping a paper trail is important as well. Candidates should make a practice of saving documents in more than one location such as on a floppy or flash drive as well as the hard drive and saving a printout of various stages of the entry as verification that all of the work is one's own.*

- *Repeatedly improved copies of the same document show the work a candidate has put into creating the entry in the event that a question arises as to a document's authorship, and provide a backup copy in the event an entry is lost in the mail. A three-ring binder or an expandable file folder for each entry is a good organizational tool for storing printouts. As a rule of thumb, floppy disks and flash drives should be stored in another location in the event of a disaster such as a break-in, fire or flood.*

Chapter Nine

PORTFOLIO ENTRY 1:
Instructional Collaboration

CHAPTER NINE AT A GLANCE

Journal Entry: January 8 92
Entry 1: Instructional Collaboration 93
Journal Entry: January 9 94
Library Media Standards Related to Entry 1 95
What Counts in This Entry 95
Documenting Collaboration 97
Table 24: Collaborative Planning Sheet 97
Journal Entry: January 10 96
Analyzing Student Work 98
Table 25: Points to Consider in Analyzing Student Work 98
Reflection on Instructional Collaboration 99
Table 26: Helpful Resources for Entry 1 99
Self-Scoring Rubric for Entry 1 100

January 8

We are back at school after the winter holidays and I have begun working with the second grade team for my collaborative lesson for Entry 1. I have taken an inventory of the resources we currently own in support of the unit they are currently studying. We have a number of suitable videotapes and nonfiction books, but our collection is a bit weak in fiction appropriate for this age. I purchased some books and a video, and also looked for some teacher resource books for our professional collection. A few teachers were able to supply some artifacts to share with students.

> *"We're all working together; that's the secret."*
> —Sam Walton

Entry 1: Instructional Collaboration

Portfolio Entry 1 is an opportunity for candidates to demonstrate evidence of partnering with a teacher or group of teachers to design, carry out, and assess student progress on an instructional sequence. Candidates should choose an instructional partner or partners carefully. Instructional collaboration denotes teamwork equally divided between certified instructors. The instructions for this entry specify collaborating with teachers to design, implement, and assess an instructional sequence. Library media specialists should play a significant role in development of all three segments—design, implementation, and assessment. The library media specialist should help design a lesson which utilizes the rich variety of resources from the media center, including, but not limited to, audio cassette tapes, videotapes and DVDs, electronic and print materials, and technology resources such as Web sites, photo libraries, and streaming audio and video clips, as well as artifacts of all sorts. Moreover, the media specialist should also play a significant role in implementation of instruction, either as a team teacher or individually with students in the classroom, lab, or media center. And, while the media specialist may not actually assign a grade, her input is valuable not only in creating an assessment tool such as a rubric, but also in evaluating how well the students utilized the media center resources associated with the lesson and how well the students participated in any instructional activities which took place in the media center or other area where she has implemented instruction.

As noted on page 50 of Information Power (1998), "…the significance of collaboration throughout the learning process is increasingly important. Collaboration is essential as library media specialists work with teachers to plan, conduct, and evaluate learning activities that incorporate information literacy." Administering a well-rounded library media program requires collaboration with many others in the learning community, including administrators and support staff like paraprofessionals, library aides, media clerks, computer lab managers, and others employed in the school system. On page 50, Information Power explains that library media specialists' collaboration with others "…is basic as they work with teachers, administrators, parents, and other members of the learning community to plan, design, and implement programs that provide access to the information that is required to meet students' and others' learning goals." It is both desirable and admirable to collaborate with parent volunteers and public librarians whenever possible, especially in obtaining resources on limited budgets. Candidates can mention the use of any of these individuals in carrying out planned activities, especially when they help distribute and organize materials, move students and equipment from place to place, and set up and take down technology, and so forth, but they probably should not be considered co-collaborators for the purpose of planning and delivering curriculum-based instruction. A helpful resource for carrying out this portfolio entry is Information Power II, particularly Chapter 3, Collaboration, Leadership and Technology.

January 9

I thought collaborating with an instructional partner would be easy, but, in fact, it was quite difficult. Normally the collaboration I do in my daily practice is brief—a teacher drops by and says something like, "We are starting the colonial period next week. Any ideas?" And I suggest some books, videos, and professional resources. I might mention that I have an activity I have used with another class to supplement classroom instruction. The classroom teacher usually says, "That's wonderful—let's do it! I'll be here tomorrow!" and our collaboration has occurred.

For this lesson, I wanted to show collaboration with a team, but I quickly realized that I would need to focus my attention on one class, because this entry requires student work samples. So, I selected two students in one second grade class as my "subjects" and began working exclusively with their teacher to complete the lesson.

Again, the problem the teacher and I encountered was finding time to plan. I rarely have any free time during the day, as I don't have a planning period. And the second grade planning time falls during our busiest stretch. We found that meeting after school wasn't always possible due to staff meetings, sick children, and other schedule conflicts, too. After we had our initial team meeting, a lot of our planning was done on the phone or by e-mail. I thought only library media specialists got to be experts at being flexible—ha! I found that this second grade teacher was extremely flexible and quite easy to work with, luckily. Sometimes, she would simply drop me a note in my box or make a comment when we passed each other in the hall. While I was surprised at how little time we had to meet at first, I found that this method of communicating actually worked very well. We were planning almost daily this way and grew to know each other's schedule as well as how to get right to the point. Everything got done, too.

Library Media Standards Related to Portfolio Entry 1

This activity relates to Standard I, Knowledge of Learners, specifically what is developmentally appropriate for students in grades pre-K through 12; Standard II, Knowledge of Teaching and Learning, particularly pedagogy related to teaching students in grades pre-K through 12 in an active learning environment and how to deliver that knowledge to students; Standard III, Knowledge of Library and Information Studies, particularly as it relates to collaborating with other instructional partners such as teachers and administrators in providing a rich instructional environment for students in grades pre-K through 12; Standard IV, Integrating Instruction, particularly as it relates to providing appropriate and varied resources and materials in support of the curriculum; Standard VI, Administering the Library Media Program, particularly as it relates to planning and managing the program so that students and staff use ideas and information effectively; and Standard VII, Reflective Practice, particularly in evaluating practice in order to increase effectiveness and student achievement.

Candidates should understand that no particular lesson is right or wrong for this entry, and there is no template to follow. Rather, candidates' portfolio entries should reflect best practices in the field that incorporate the standards. Candidates should consider what activities and resources the media center can provide that would promote an age-appropriate, active learning environment for the students in this particular class, as well as what information literacy skills relate to this instructional sequence, and how instruction on these skills should be designed, implemented, and evaluated for maximum effect.

Candidates should demonstrate proficiency in linking the resources of a library media program to a particular curricular area and to collaborate with a colleague to provide appropriate instruction in that area. This entry requires documentation in student work samples.

What Counts in This Entry

What counts in this entry is ongoing collaboration, interwoven with appropriate resources from the library media program. Resources can be in the form of personnel, print materials, technology, services, and so on. Candidates should consider the current resources available in support of the instructional sequence to be taught and consider what items might update and enhance the curriculum if funds are available to purchase them. If funds are not available, candidates may work with another school or public library to obtain items through an interlibrary loan. Some districts and state departments also provide materials on loan that candidates can obtain for staff and students. Of course online resources can be a strong component of any instructional unit. Library media specialists can play a role in evaluating specific Web sites and other online resources such as streaming video for age appropriateness, correlation to curriculum standards and authority, accuracy, currency, and validity. Candidates should indicate the role they played in obtaining and recommending appropriate resources for this instructional sequence. Candidates might work closely with other school libraries to preview materials that could make good additions to a collection when funds are available, or consider previewing items under consideration from vendors for a brief period of time.

January 10

This lesson is really coming together! I have located a number of professional resources and have created an exciting lesson that involves a technology project. The students will be researching topics in the media center for facts to include in their project. We have scheduled the classes in advance and have worked out a rubric for scoring their work.

I chose a second grade boy and a girl whose work samples I will include with my portfolio entry. As I wanted to show growth over time, I thought that these students would be getting a great deal of my attention and should show significant growth once they had accomplished their assignment.

I am keeping a log of the times their teacher and I collaborate on our plans for this lesson. A lot of planning has been done on the fly! She leaves me notes in my box and I e-mail her back. But that is working pretty well for us.

Documenting Collaboration

Candidates should carefully document ongoing planning sessions, decisions jointly made, activities carried out, student progress, and what worked or didn't work in this sequence. Keeping a log of planning sessions would be beneficial. Denote which of the partners contributed and what the specific contribution was. If planning is done on the fly, as it often is, note that as well. Planning can occur in many forms. While a face-to-face meeting would be most appropriate initially, future meetings can be by phone or e-mail, through notes exchanged in mailboxes, in the hall, as well as formal sit-down planning sessions. Keep a record of all exchanges made during any of these types of planning sessions. Save copies of any e-mail, or keep journal entries after meetings on the fly. A daily log entry might save time and frustration in recreating these ongoing planning sessions.

Table 24

Collaborative Planning Sheet

Date	Meeting Location	Planners Present	Purpose/Goals/Tasks

Analyzing Student Work

Student work should be thoroughly and thoughtfully analyzed. Analysis of student work can be either independent or collaborative. Media specialists should play a key role in designing a rubric or other means of assessment for evaluating student work. Assessment should include student performance using resources from the media center and interaction during the instruction provided by the media specialist. While the media specialist may not actually score students, as a member of the team, she should be given an opportunity to discuss and evaluate student performance with other instructional partners.

Candidates should show evidence of setting high but appropriate goals for student learning, addressing multiple learning styles, providing a rich variety of materials, and connecting multiple aspects of information literacy into instruction. Certainly the rich variety of resources available should help candidates to address multiple learning styles. But if multiple resources are available in support of visual learners but limited numbers of resources are available for auditory or kinesthetic learners, this could be an indicator of items the media specialist might consider purchasing for the collection.

In analyzing student work samples, candidates should, first of all, consider the goals of the activity and the student growth exhibited over time. In addition, candidates should seek to identify examples of student growth as a result of the assignment. They should also compare the student work sample to the curriculum standard. Candidates should ask, "Does the student work sample indicate that the student is aware of the standard and expectations for meeting that standard?" Candidates should look for evidence that the student has followed directions and seek concrete examples of student comprehension of the content material. Finally, candidates should consider the way students solved problems they encountered as they worked. Analysis should provide evidence that the candidate is not only aware of how to best deliver the content material to the students but also how to manage and monitor student learning effectively.

Table 25

Points to Consider in Analyzing Student Work

- *Set high but appropriate goals for student work.*
- *Consider using collaborative assessment of student work.*
- *Create a rubric or similar assessment tool for scoring.*
- *Seek evidence of growth from the beginning to the end of the assignment.*
- *Compare the student work to the standards used in planning the assignment.*
- *Look for evidence of comprehension of the material covered.*
- *Uncover any problems students encountered in completing the assignment and how they were solved.*
- *Thoughtfully comment on student performance and growth.*
- *Prescribe steps for improvement.*
- *Reflect on areas of instruction that need refinement.*

Fast Fact:

For more tips on analyzing student work, see **Information Power (1998) Appendix E: Student Performance Assessment on pages 173-182**.

Reflection on Instructional Collaboration

Finally, reflection on what worked and what didn't work well in this instructional sequence should provide insight into segments that should be continued in the future as well as areas of weakness that might be improved in future learning activities. Reflection can involve thoughts and insight from the instructional partner or partners in this sequence. Reflection should consider the successful as well as the not so successful activities and events. While everyone would like to consider their instruction to be effective, no one is perfect. Each one of us has room for improvement. The idea of reflecting on instruction is to continuously seek to improve and thereby more effectively produce student-learning gains. Comments from parents and students add richness and depth into the effectiveness of the instructional sequence. And reflection from an administrator or instructional lead teacher who has observed or been aware of these activities is valuable also.

Table 26

Helpful Resources for Entry 1

Roles of the Library Media Specialist: Instructional Partner
http://www.bcps.org/offices/lis/office/partner.html

www.ala.org/ala/acrl/aboutacrl/acrlchapters/chaptertopics/ctv19n2.pdf

ALA Collaboration PowerPoint
http://www.ala.org/ala/aasl/aboutaasl/aaslgovernance/aaslpres/iowa-workingtogether.ppt

NCREL Notes & Reflections: Issue 5 Summer/Fall, 2003, Teacher Collaboration Supports Instructional Change; Collaboration Harnesses the Energy of Change
http://www.ncrel.org/info/notes/fall03/change.htm

ERIC Clearinghouse Collaboration Documents List
http://ericec.org/faq/regsped.html

www.cusd.chico.k12.ca.us/~pmilbury/ttt.links.html

www.eduscapes.com/sms/collaboration.html

www.es.houstonisd.org/scogginsES/information/library/collabor.htm

www.indianalearns.org/collaborativespecial.asp

www.nashville-schools.davidson.k12.tn.us/TIPSmanual/planningsheets.html

Self-Scoring Rubric for Entry 1

Candidates can self-score their entries to check for thoroughness and rich detail. For each question below:

- score a 4 if you have provided "clear, consistent, and convincing evidence"
- score a 3 if you have provided "clear evidence"
- score a 2 if you have provided "limited evidence"
- score a 1 if you have provided "little or no evidence"

Have you regularly collaborated with a certified teacher and other members of the learning community to provide a curriculum-related instructional sequence that is developmentally appropriate and integrates information literacy?

4   3   2   1

Have you utilized a rich variety of developmentally appropriate resources from the media center to support and enhance instruction?

4   3   2   1

Did you associate a curriculum area with an activity involving multimedia and information literacy instruction?

4   3   2   1

Have you, as media specialist, played a key role in developing, implementing, and evaluating the instructional sequence?

4   3   2   1

Did you provide evidence of collaboratively establishing high and worthwhile goals in this instructional sequence?

4   3   2   1

Have you provided student work samples consistent with what you say you have done in your written entry?

4   3   2   1

Have you given a written description of the materials, resources, and activities you provided in support of this instructional sequence that are a reflection of the library media standards?

4   3   2   1

Have you thoroughly analyzed student work samples as they relate to the instructional sequence and the goals/objectives of that instructional sequence, particularly as they relate to activities implemented in the media center?

4   3   2   1

Have you reflected on the instructional collaboration in this instructional sequence? How could you more effectively collaborate with an instructional partner in the future? How could you more effectively collaborate with parents, community partners, and public librarians to provide resources to support instruction?

4   3   2   1

Overall, does your entry provide clear, consistent, and convincing evidence of instructional collaboration to enhance a curriculum objective?

4   3   2   1

Chapter Ten

PORTFOLIO ENTRY 2: Appreciation of Literature

CHAPTER TEN AT A GLANCE

Journal Entry: January 20 ....
Library Media Standards Related to Entry 2 ....
What Counts in Entry 2 ....
Journal Entry: January 30 ....
Table 27: Brainstorming for Ways to
Stimulate Student Appreciation of Literature ....
Table 28: Helpful Resources for Entry 2 ....
Self-Scoring Rubric for Entry 2 ....

January 20

I am working with a fourth grade teacher on my literature appreciation unit. She is very enthusiastic and has recently completed district training on the balanced literacy approach. While her class is not skilled at making inferences, they are familiar with the process and have begun implementing it in the classroom.

I know that this class presents a number of academic challenges due to the size, diversity of the group, and the wide range of ability levels, but I think that the integration of technology will help us overcome some of them. What worries me about this entry is how to effectively demonstrate evidence of the inviting atmosphere of my media center and my efforts to provide a collection that meets the needs of our learners and the curriculum.

Also, I have been having trouble making my two-minute pan and don't know how my lesson video will turn out!

> *"There is no Frigate like a Book, to take us Lands away,
> nor any Coursers like a Page of prancing poetry…"*
>
> —Emily Dickinson

Library Media Standards Related to Entry 2

Portfolio Entry 2 is an opportunity for candidates to demonstrate evidence of their ability to provide equal access to all students, to create an inviting atmosphere in their library media center, and to cultivate their students' skill in making appropriate inferences and interpretations of literature. This activity relates to Standard I, Knowledge of Learners; Standard II, Knowledge of Teaching and Learning; Standard III, Knowledge of Library and Information Studies; Standard VI, Administering the Library Media Program; Standard VII, Reflective Practice; and Standard IX, Ethics, Equity, and Diversity.

Candidates should demonstrate proficiency in establishing a library media center collection that is solidly based on both the curriculum and the abilities, needs, and interests of the learners, and is readily accessible and attractive to all. Candidates should also demonstrate an ability to creatively connect literature to a content area lesson, and effectively guide students to make thoughtful inferences and interpretations of that literature. Candidates should understand that no particular lesson is right or wrong for this entry, and there is no template to follow. Rather, candidates' portfolio entries should reflect best practices in the field that incorporates the standards.

What Counts in Entry 2

What counts in this lesson is explicit evidence of an ability to relate literature to a content area in an integrated learning activity that clearly addresses the needs, interests, and abilities of the students involved, while at the same time creatively challenges them to make insightful connections between that literature and their curriculum in an environment that is attractive to them, and accessible to all. Candidates should create a two-minute videotape of their media center showing the areas they have featured to promote reading and literature appreciation, and a fifteen-minute videotape of instruction that demonstrates lively student-to-teacher interaction and student-to-student interaction, which helps readers to value and deeply comprehend content-related literature.

Candidates will submit a seventeen-minute videotape that includes a two-minute pan of the media center and highlights the arrangement of materials to make them attractive to students. The pan should circle the entire media center, and is designed to provide a visual representation of the ways the media specialist works to make the environment user-friendly and inviting to students. The pan should highlight special collections and interesting displays, as well as represent the overall layout of

January 30

I am stressing out over the activity I want to implement for Portfolio Entry 2. I am excited about working with this fourth grade class, though. The teacher has been practicing a balanced literacy approach in her classroom, so the students have not had too much trouble making inferences. The teacher is already trying some other balanced literacy strategies in her classroom.

I have completed my work with the students and have begun writing the rough draft of this portfolio entry. I need to send it off to my proofreader and see what she has to say about this entry.

The activities we did in making inferences were successful so I am planning on trying them out with other groups of students.

the media center and of special areas, such as a story corner or reading nook, that serve to attract students. The remainder of the videotape should include a fifteen-minute segment that demonstrates how the media specialist stimulates student interest in literature and enhances student learning through inference and interpretation of literature that relates to a specific content area.

Candidates may consider selecting literature that connects to a specific content area and design strategies to help stimulate students' interest in such literature. Literature that relates to an art, music, social studies or science unit, for example, is appropriate for the purpose of this lesson. Any activity, such as an interactive Web site on the piece of literature, or an interview with the author of the piece, or even a video clip of the selection, can be effective in activating student interest. As Information Power (1998) states, "Strong and imaginative activities that promote reading have always been a staple of program offerings, and over the years the program's focus has expanded to promote critical viewing and listening skills as well. These core abilities of reading, viewing, and listening, along with writing and communication, form the basis for developing information literacy skills that are equally basic for today's students."

Candidates may create their own promotional material by doing a booktalk, creating a multimedia presentation on a book or author, reciting a poem from a book or particular author, or dressing as a character in a curriculum-related book. Information Power goes on to advise library media specialists to "..model the effective and enthusiastic use of books, videos, films, multimedia, and other creative expressions of information as sources of pleasure and information." Candidates are not limited to the suggestions given, the genres mentioned, or the subject areas listed. Any curriculum area could be enhanced by the use of related literature.

Table 27

Brainstorming for Ways to Enhance Student Appreciation of Literature

- What types of presentations of new books have you used effectively in the past in promoting literature to students?
- In what ways have students successfully promoted literature to their peers?
- What Web sites effectively stimulate interest in authors and literature?
- What software might be used to stimulate student interest in literature?
- In what ways can you use distribution systems in your school to advertise literature in a way that stimulates student interest?
- What student or visiting performer presentations have effectively stimulated interest in literature?
- What book report formats have stimulated student interest in literature?
- What promotional materials have you successfully used to promote student interest in literature?
- What media can you show that effectively stimulates student interest in literature?
- What school-based publications would be suitable for publishing literature promotions?
- What resources are available in your community to promote student interest in literature?
- In what ways have teachers in your school effectively promoted literature with their students?

Table 28

Helpful Resources for Entry 2

From Assessor to Candidate: An Inside Look! by Natalie Lindsay on the AASL Web Site
http://www.ala.org/ala/aasl/aaslpubsandjournals/kqweb/kqarchives/vol32/lindsay.htm

Backflip
http://www.backflip.com/members/librarymedia/11786139

Carol Hurst's Children's Literature Site
www.carolhurst.com

Literature Circles
http://www.literaturecircles.com/

Reading Lady
http://www.readinglady.com/

NEA's Best Bet Book List
http://www.nea.org/webresources/bestbooklinks.html

Glandon, S. 2000. *Caldecott Connections to Science.* Libraries Unlimited.

Hurst, C., et. al. 1999. *Curriculum Connections: Picture Books in Grades 3 and Up.* Linworth Publishing, Inc.

Keane, N. and Walt, C. 2002. *Teaching Science through Literature.* Linworth Publishing, Inc.

Keane, N. and Walt, C. 2002. *Teaching Social Studies through Literature.* Linworth Publishing, Inc.

Miller, D. 2004. *The Standards-Based Integrated Library.* Linworth Publishing, Inc.

Weissman, A. 2001. *Transforming Storytimes into Reading and Writing Lessons.* Linworth Publishing, Inc.

Self-Scoring Rubric for Entry 2

Candidates can self-score their entries to check for thoroughness and rich detail.
For each question below:

- score a 4 if you have provided "clear, consistent, and convincing evidence"
- score a 3 if you have provided "clear evidence"
- score a 2 if you have provided "limited evidence"
- score a 1 if you have provided "little or no evidence"

Did you provide evidence of establishing an inviting environment in your school library media center?

4   3   2   1

Did you show how your collection strongly supports the curriculum and meets the needs, interest, and abilities of your staff and students?

4   3   2   1

Did you demonstrate how you have promoted specific areas of your media center to foster an appreciation of literature?

4   3   2   1

Did you plan your instruction so as to meet the diverse needs, interests, and abilities of your students?

4   3   2   1

Did you model for and encourage your students to make thoughtful interpretations and inferences with a piece or pieces of literature?

4   3   2   1

Did you show how you creatively connected literature to a content area?

4   3   2   1

Did you thoroughly analyze your instruction, including your rationale for including the select pieces of literature, as well as why you felt they supported the curriculum area you chose?

4   3   2   1

Did you reflect on your instruction so as to define any weak areas and set positive goals for improvement in the future?

4   3   2   1

Did your two-minute pan focus on how you highlighted specific areas of your media center to foster appreciation of literature?

4   3   2   1

Did your fifteen-minute videotape demonstrate active student engagement in making inferences and interpretations of a content-related piece of literature?

4   3   2   1

In this entry, did you clearly, consistently, and convincingly demonstrate how you fostered an appreciation of literature in your students?

4   3   2   1

Chapter Eleven

PORTFOLIO ENTRY 3:
Integrating Technology

CHAPTER ELEVEN AT A GLANCE
Journal Entry: February 2 110
Library Media Standards Related to Entry 3 111
What Counts in Entry 3 111
Journal Entry: February 5 112
Instructional Materials 113
*Table 29: Brainstorming for Technologies
to Incorporate into a Lesson for Entry 3* 113
Journal Entry: February 15 114
*Table 30: Brainstorming for Student
Technology Projects for Entry 3* 115
Table 31: Helpful Resources for Entry 3 115
Self-Scoring Rubric for Entry 3 116

February 2

I am working on a technology integration lesson for Entry 3. The students have been researching a variety of subjects and are creating presentations with their research. My job now is to assist them in ethically utilizing the technology resources we have available to complete their presentations.

I am proud of the good job they have done and hope to see their work once it is finished!

> *"Obviously everyone wants to be successful, but I want to be looked back on as being very innovative, very trusted and ethical and ultimately making a big difference in the world."*
>
> —Sergey Brin

Library Media Standards Related to Entry 3

Portfolio Entry 3 is an opportunity for candidates to demonstrate evidence of their ability to effectively integrate technologies into an instructional sequence while promoting the ethical and legal use of information in students' research. This activity relates to Standard I, Knowledge of Learners; Standard II, Knowledge of Teaching and Learning; Standard III, Knowledge of Library and Information Studies; Standard IV, Integrating Instruction; Standard V, Leading Innovation Through the Library Media Program; Standard VII, Reflective Practice; and Standard IX, Ethics, Equity, and Diversity. Candidates should understand that no particular lesson is right or wrong for this entry and there is no template to follow. Rather, candidates' portfolio entries should reflect best practices in the field that incorporates the standards.

What Counts in Entry 3

What counts in this entry is the candidate's evidence of facilitating a rich and thorough understanding of the student's use of technologies to make decisions, solve problems, obtain information ethically and legally, and produce work with that information. Candidates will submit a twenty-minute videotape (in two unedited ten-minute segments) showing how they effectively selected and integrated specific technologies into a content-area lesson, and how they promoted student understanding of the ethical and legal use of information.

Like Entry 2, this entry requires candidates to submit a videotape of a lesson implemented to incorporate technology and foster student comprehension of the implications of ethical and legal use of the information they gather. Videotapes should be in two segments of approximately ten minutes each. Each segment should be made with the same class involved in the same lesson and must not involve any editing or special effects. The first segment should provide evidence of effective use of technology in a whole group setting, while the second segment should show the candidate's work with small groups or individuals as they interact with technologies to demonstrate understanding of ethical and legal use of information.

February 5

Gosh! I thought making the videotape for this lesson was going to be easy, but it was a disaster. I had to reschedule my session with the multiage class a couple of times, and when I finally gave up and taped the class anyway, there was banging in the background from our network installers and I was afraid to use the tape. I was really disappointed, too, because the lesson was exactly what I had hoped for otherwise.

I ended up starting over completely with another class doing a collaborative lesson on the laptop computers, but was disappointed in the quality of the lesson and the students' response to it. The tape went well, but the lesson did not fully demonstrate the things I had hoped to show about ethical use of information. Most likely the result was due to the fact that I hadn't had sufficient time to plan with the classroom teacher in order to carry this out well.

I ended up going back to the original lesson and using the video anyway, although I thought the background noise might count against me. Of course, I didn't have any editing of the tape or anything else that would have made it unacceptable. I just worried that the students wouldn't be totally focused with all the disruptions. In final analysis, I actually found that I was more distracted by the noise than the students were.

Instructional Materials

A list of instructional materials used should be submitted with this portfolio entry. For the purpose of this lesson, instructional materials may include items such as Web sites, guidelines for the proper use of information, citation instructions, digital images, videotapes, and so on. Any instructional transparencies or items written on a board or projected with multimedia may be photographed or videotaped for the assessors.

Candidate's lessons should involve whole group instruction and instruction given in small groups or individually, and should actively engage students in problem-solving, gathering information, producing a product with that information, and communicating the results. The use of technology should not be the primary focus of the lesson, but should be used as a tool for facilitating ethical and legal use of information. Appropriately selected technologies for this instructional activity should demonstrate a candidate's ability to engage students and to enhance their understanding of the ethical and legal use of information. On page 54, Information Power (1998) clarifies the role of the media specialist in the integration of technology into instruction this way: "Acting as a technologist (rather than a technician) and a collaborator with teachers, the library media specialist plays a critical role in designing student experiences that focus on authentic learning, information literacy, and curricular mastery—not simply on manipulating machinery."

Technology may include, but is not limited to, videotapes, streaming video, computer software, hardware and peripherals, multimedia, Web sites, databases, closed circuit television, cable television, and satellite broadcasts. Students might demonstrate their understanding of the ethical use of information by creating a digital project such as an Inspiration web, a PowerPoint presentation, a Hyperstudio presentation, a Web page, a digital video, a timeline, or other multimedia project in which they include information they have ethically and legally used.

Table 29

Brainstorming for Technologies to Incorporate into a Lesson for Entry 3

Which of the following technologies do you have access to and use regularly in your school:

- *Videotapes?*
- *Streaming video?*
- *Computer software?*
- *Digital cameras?*
- *Digital camcorders?*
- *Whiteboards?*
- *Multimedia projectors?*
- *Assistive technology?*
- *Web sites?*
- *Databases?*
- *Closed circuit television?*
- *Cable television?*
- *Satellite broadcasts?*
- *Computer hardware and peripherals?*

February 15

The students have finished their research. They are excited about creating presentation projects. Each student is required to include their list of resources used. We will be showing their presentations next week. I am proud of the good job they have done and hope we can save these for future reference.

Table 30

Brainstorming for Student Technology Projects for Entry 3
Which of the following could you comfortably facilitate for an Entry 3 lesson?

- *Video production?*
- *Digital video production?*
- *Inspiration webs?*
- *Hyperstudio multimedia presentations?*
- *PowerPoint Presentations?*
- *Web pages?*
- *Timelines?*
- *Digital books?*

Table 31

Helpful Resources for Entry 3

Forest, D. and M. 2001. Becoming an accomplished teacher in the 21st century. *Edutopia Magazine* online. Retrieved 4/2/05 from the URL: http://www.edutopia.org/php/article.php?id=Art_737

Glandon, S. 2003. *Integrating Technology: Effective Tools for Collaboration.* Libraries Unlimited. *Information Power: Building Partnerships for Learning. 1998.* American Library Association, p. 54.

Johnson, D. 2003. *Learning Right from Wrong in the Digital Age: An Ethics Guide for Parents, Teachers, Librarians and Others Who Care About Computer-Using Young People.* Linworth Publishing, Inc.

Johnson, D. and Simpson, C. 2005. "Are you the copy cop?" *Learning and Leading with Technology.* International Society for Technology in Education, 32 (7), 14-20.

Langran, E, Langra, R. & Bull, G. 2005. "Copyright Law and Technology." *Learning and Leading with Technology.* International Society for Technology in Education, 32 (7), 24-26.

Scribner, M. "Defeating plagiarism in the Information Age." *Library Media Connection,* (21) 5, 32-34.

Simpson, C. 2001. *Copyright for Schools: A Practical Guide, Third Edition.* Linworth Publishing, Inc.

Simpson, C. 2003. *Ethics in School Librarianship.* Linworth Publishing, Inc.

Thompson, K. 2005. "Copyright 101." *Learning and Leading with Technology.* International Society for Technology in Education, 32 (7), 10-12.

Self-Scoring Rubric for Portfolio Entry 3

- score a 4 if you have provided "clear, consistent, and convincing evidence"
- score a 3 if you have provided "clear evidence"
- score a 2 if you have provided "limited evidence"
- score a 1 if you have provided "little or no evidence"

Did you plan a technology-rich lesson that demonstrates how you provide equal access to information for all learners?

    4   3   2   1

Did you foster critical thinking and information literacy skills in your instructional sequence?

    4   3   2   1

Did you preserve the confidentiality of information requests while adhering to laws regarding citation of information and fair use of information throughout all media?

    4   3   2   1

Did you enhance and enrich classroom instruction with technology resources?

    4   3   2   1

Did you demonstrate how you advise students in efficient research strategies and engage students so as to deepen their learning experiences?

    4   3   2   1

Did you model ethical use of information for your students and advise students in the application of the most current ethical practices in use of information?

    4   3   2   1

Did you demonstrate a commitment to lifelong learning?

    4   3   2   1

Overall, did you plan and implement an instructional sequence that effectively demonstrates ethical use of information resources and technologies in support of classroom instruction?

    4   3   2   1

Chapter Twelve

PORTFOLIO ENTRY 4:
Documented Accomplishments

CHAPTER TWELVE AT A GLANCE

Journal Entry: February 22 118
Library Media Standards Related to Entry 4 119
What Counts in Entry 4 119
Journal Entry: February 25 120
What is an Accomplishment? 119
What Accomplishments Count? 121
Table 32: Brainstorming for Types of Accomplishments that Link to Student Achievement 121
Linking to Student Achievement 123
What Documents Matter? 123
Journal Entry: March 3 122
How to Reflect on Accomplishments 123
Description and Analysis of Accomplishments 123
Table 33: Helpful Resources for Entry 4 124
Self-Scoring Rubric for Entry 4 125

February 22

I have been reading of the accomplishments of others on the e-mail list and I am amazed at the number and extent of activities that other media specialists have voluntarily pursued! As a group, media specialists are some of the hardest working and most dedicated professionals I know. I have read of media specialists becoming PTA officers, serving on the school board, teaching college classes, leading staff development programs, hosting evening and weekend hours to serve the community, and much more. I need to find out what types of accomplishments should be included in my portfolio entry and then see what I have done that qualifies as an accomplishment.

> *"It doesn't matter who you are, where you come from. The ability to triumph begins with you. Always."*
> —Oprah Winfrey

Library Media Standards Related to Entry 4

Portfolio Entry 4 is an opportunity for candidates to demonstrate their contributions to student learning, their professional growth, and their leadership within the learning community. These activities relate to Standard VIII, Professional Growth; and Standard X, Leadership, Advocacy, and Community Partnerships. Candidates should understand that no accomplishment is right or wrong for this entry and there is no template to follow. Rather, candidates' accomplishments should reflect best practices in the field that incorporates the standards.

What Counts in Entry 4

What counts in this entry is the candidate's evidence of enhancing student achievement through work with families and community partners, work with colleagues and other professionals, and work on self-improvement. Candidates will submit documentation of their interactive communication with families to enhance student learning, their goal-oriented professional growth to improve their own instruction and student learning, and their leadership in the professional learning community to help others and promote positive change to improve student achievement.

What is an Accomplishment?

An accomplishment is an achievement that goes beyond what is required of regular staff and faculty. For example, every certified teacher is required to register for staff development courses periodically. This would not be an accomplishment, as it is required of everyone. But, if a teacher notices that her class is struggling with making inferences and registers for a special training session on fostering students' ability to make inferences, even though she has completed her staff development requirements, that would be an accomplishment, as it goes beyond what is required of her. Accomplishments could include seeking another degree, scheduling specific staff development courses to meet the needs of students, attending conferences related to curricular areas, obtaining training in order to learn a new skill, developing a new program, speaking at a conference or offering training to others, publishing materials, and so on.

February 25

I have continued to stay active in my field, seeking training in areas of interest and continuing to earn degrees. But I am having a hard time determining which of these activities might be considered accomplishments. I thought that I had achieved some level of accomplishment in my field, but now I am confused about what amounts to accomplishment. And I am wondering how I can show that the things I have done have impacted student achievement. Since I don't have a specific group of students assigned to me, I am wondering how I can effectively link my accomplishments to improved student achievement.

What Accomplishments Count?

For the purpose of Entry 4, accomplishments should fall into one of three categories: work with families and communities, work as a leader and collaborator, and work as a learner. Work with families and communities includes not only those families directly related to the students candidates serve, but also those in the wider community in which candidates work. This interaction should show two-way, interactive communication. Web pages and newsletters, for example, are great means of getting the word out on news and services available in library media programs, but they generally do not foster two-way, interactive communication, unless candidates send out a survey in their newsletters, or e-mail news directly to parents and community members, and maintain dialog as a result. Web pages, likewise, do not foster two-way communication, unless they provide a link for e-mail and ongoing e-mail dialog results. A better means of communicating could be through hosting an event such as a forum that invites questions and answers from parents and community members, or opening one evening for a curriculum-related storytelling hour, giving tours and conferences with families and community members afterward. Work as a leader and collaborator includes those local, state, or national activities in which candidates have participated over the past five years such as presenting at conferences, hosting staff training, teaching courses, or publishing materials. Work as a learner includes those professional growth activities in which candidates have participated over the past five years for gaining expertise directly related to the library media field. In selecting accomplishments to document, candidates should reflect on those that directly support the standards and clearly show a link to improved student achievement. Candidates must document specific accomplishments in all three areas.

Table 32

Brainstorming for Types of Accomplishments that Link to Student Achievement

Have you been involved in any of the following:

- *Leading a technology staff development program?*
- *Designing a course that links library media resources to curriculum standards?*
- *Teaching a technology course to teachers?*
- *Training parents to use local online resources?*
- *Training students to head a tech help team?*
- *Presenting a program you created at your school at a local, state, or national conference?*
- *Taking a course on balanced literacy strategies to help student make inferences from literature?*
- *Taking a course on setting up a library media blog for your community?*
- *Taking a course on online resources used in your media program?*
- *Training to be a webmaster for your school library media center Web page?*
- *Training to be a technology support specialist for your school media center?*
- *Offering an after-school homework help program?*
- *Creating a summer reading program?*
- *Offering a weekly story hour and checkout program during the summer?*
- *Collaborating with your local public library or bookstore to secure storytellers and authors in your school?*

March 3

I have nearly completed my Portfolio Entry 4 and am reflecting on my accomplishments as a whole. Entry 4 requires a reflective summary on my accomplishments and their impact on student achievement. I am not sure how to show a direct link to student achievement, since I don't have a group of students assigned specifically to me.

Linking to Student Achievement

Accomplishments that are significant, or beyond the ordinary, are good choices if they meet the criteria listed above and relate to an increase in student achievement. For library media specialists, showing improvement in student achievement directly may not be possible. Library media specialists may not have test scores or grades, for example, to compare in relation to an achievement. But indirect links to student achievement should be clear. For example, holding a storytime at a local bookstore may not relate directly to student achievement at a local school, but holding a story hour in the school library each week during the summer and offering checkout times afterward would. The library media specialist could keep records of the attendance at the event and the circulation that results afterward. The implication is that student reading achievement at the school would be improved as a result of this event.

What Documents Matter?

Documents that can provide first-hand evidence of a candidate's accomplishments are the very effective. Certificates of course completion, registration papers, conference programs and flyers, especially with a candidate's name on them, are good to submit as evidence. In the absence of such documentation, candidates may submit a National Board Verification Form (included with portfolio instructions) whereby an administrator, supervisor, department head, or coworker can attest to their accomplishments as stated in the entry.

Description and Analysis of Accomplishments

For each accomplishment included in Entry 4, candidates should give a detailed description of the accomplishment within the candidate's specific teaching context. The description should avoid acronyms and abbreviations and should be clear enough to link to the documentation submitted as verification of the accomplishment. Candidates should also give an explanation of why the accomplishment is significant and what impact it has had on student achievement as a result. Each description and analysis should relate to a single accomplishment.

How to Reflect on Accomplishments

Once candidates have completed the description and analysis for each accomplishment, they should write a reflective summary of the accomplishments as a group. This reflection should note any patterns or trends within the series of accomplishments and give detail on how these accomplishments as a group impact student achievement. For example, the reflection should note what accomplishments worked well for a candidate's specific community, and what might have worked even better with a few changes. Candidates should reflect on meeting specific needs of specific groups of students at a specific point in time.

Table 33

Helpful Resources for Entry 4

National Board Question and Answer Page for Documented Accomplishments
https://nbpts3.ets.org/cis/faq0405/documentedaccomplishments.html

NEA Guide to Professional Growth
http://www.nea.org/profdev/index.htmlx

ALA's Research Report on School Librarians as Leaders
http://www.ala.org/ala/aasl/aaslpubsandjournals/slmrb/slmrcontents/volume52002/shannon.htm#conclusions

Johnson, D. 1999. "Putting the Horse back before the cart: technology skills for educational leaders."
http://www.doug-johnson.com/handouts/cart.pdf.

Loertscher, D, and Achterman, D. 2002. *Increasing academic achievement through the Library Media Center.* Hi Willow Research and Publishing.

Miller, N. 2003. *Impact! Documenting the LMC program for accountability.* Hi Willow Research & Publishing.

Self-Scoring Rubric for Entry 4

- score a 4 if you have provided "clear, consistent, and convincing evidence"
- score a 3 if you have provided "clear evidence"
- score a 2 if you have provided "limited evidence"
- score a 1 if you have provided "little or no evidence"

Have you documented clear evidence of reaching out to students' families and community through interactive communications from your media center?

(4)   (3)   (2)   (1)

Does your communication focus on teaching and learning issues and student progress as a result of your media center programs?

(4)   (3)   (2)   (1)

Have you documented work as a learner to improve your teaching and student learning within your own practice?

(4)   (3)   (2)   (1)

Have you sought opportunities to learn skills you need to improve student achievement within your own practice?

(4)   (3)   (2)   (1)

Have you documented work as a leader among your colleagues to improve teaching and learning within your district, state, or nation?

(4)   (3)   (2)   (1)

Have you documented work you have done as a leader to share your expertise with others to improve student learning?

(4)   (3)   (2)   (1)

Have you reflected on trends or patterns you see emerging from your accomplishments that have had an impact on student learning in your situation?

(4)   (3)   (2)   (1)

Chapter Thirteen

ONLINE ASSESSMENT Tips

CHAPTER THIRTEEN AT A GLANCE

Journal Entry: April 5 128
Overview of the Online Assessment 129
Journal Entry: April 10 130
Assessment Center Tips 129
How to Study for the Online Assessment 131
Table 34: Assessment Center KWL 132
Helpful Resources for the Online Assessment 133

April 5

I thought that being an assessor might be helpful to me in achieving certification for myself, but I have realized now that I have had to earn it all by myself. Being an assessor helped me have a better understanding of the process, but that can be achieved with a good mentor and having a clear picture of the expectations for each entry.

I am thinking that the online assessment will be the hardest part for me. I am not a good test taker, especially when my work is timed. What if my mind goes blank?

I am going to ask others in my group what they think about preparing for the online assessment.

*"Success comes from having dreams
that are bigger than your fears."*

—Terry Litwiller

Overview of the Online Assessment

The Online Assessment is a written test of pedagogical knowledge in the library media field. The six entries are essay questions testing candidates on areas considered by practicing media specialists and experts in the field to be among the most important areas of accomplishment. The six areas are organizational management, ethical and legal tenets, technologies, collection development, information literacy, and knowledge of literature.

While the questions are not known ahead of time, a variety of resources are available to help prepare for them. Sample questions are available so that candidates can time themselves and practice responding to questions written in a similar format.

Candidates are allowed thirty minutes to respond to each question and may move forward but not back. If the timed response format is intimidating, candidates may find it helpful to anticipate typical questions that might be asked of them for each assessment area and prepare to write an essay on that subject. It may also be helpful to practice typing a response while timing your work in thirty-minute segments.

As with the SAT and other high-stakes tests, the actual test questions may vary slightly while still applying to the same subject. Without knowing the questions being asked, the most a candidate can do is to have a broad and deep knowledge of each subject area and become familiar with the test site and the computer-based format to eliminate stress caused by unfamiliarity.

Assessment Center Tips

- *Go through all ten standards thoroughly and know them well. Pull out significant words and phrases in each standard and think of ways that you exemplify them in your daily practice.*
- *Read the scoring guide and rubric to see what is important in each of the six exercises. Make sure you understand what items characterize a level 4 and a level 3 response.*
- *Visit the NBPTS.org assessment center orientation at http://www.nbpts.org/candidates/acob/.*
- *Take the practice online assessment at http://www.nbpts.org/candidates/tutorial.cfm.*
- *Prepare some sample questions on each subject area and practice responding to them in a timed format. Memorize general responses to each subject and practice typing them quickly and accurately.*

# April 10

I found it helpful to visit the site a few days before the actual test. It was a good thing I did, too, as I almost missed it. The sign was rather nondescript although it was located in the center of a small shopping area.

Visiting the site ahead of time helped me time myself in morning traffic so that I would arrive in plenty of time on the day of the test. Also, visiting in advance allowed me to gauge the temperature of the room, which was quite cold. I brought a sweater on the day of the test and found that it helped me to be more comfortable. The chilly test room would have been distracting otherwise. By visiting the site in advance I was also able to get a feel for the test environment. The computers were located in study carrels side by side along a wall and the room they were in was rather long and narrow. I realized that headphones would be a good idea to drown out extraneous noise as we were all seated rather close to each other. I also realized that there wasn't much space on the desktop for jotting down my thoughts before writing. I used some half sheets of paper for jotting down my thoughts before I began the actual timed test.

- *Discuss the six subject areas with other media specialists and ask them how they would respond to the prompts. Use the best responses to formulate your own.*

- *Visit the assessment center ahead of time and check out the layout of the room, the seating, the temperature, and so on. Familiarize yourself so that you will not be distracted on test day. Locate the restrooms, water fountains, administrator's desk, and so on. Time yourself driving to the center so that you can allow adequate time, even in rush hour traffic.*

- *Visit the American Library Association's Web site and print out materials relating to specific areas such as reconsiderations, ethical and legal use of information, advocacy, information literacy, and administration.*

- *Memorize the steps in the information problem-solving model you use with your students. Be able to cite examples of how you implement it.*

- *Plan a situation that calls for significant collection development above and beyond what you already have. Choose an area of weakness in your own collection and tell the details of how you would go about the process of building the collection in that area and why you selected what you did. Be very specific.*

- *Become very familiar with award-winning pieces of literature appropriate for support of a curricular area you teach. Practice designing lessons to enhance the teaching of a lesson using a specific piece of literature.*

- *Consider a situation in which your expertise in media center technologies might be required. Propose a solution that articulates the hardware, software, and connectivity requirements to implement the plan. Evaluate the issues you might be facing in each area.*

How to Study for the Online Assessment

Some candidates feel that it is impossible to study for the online assessment as it tests your working knowledge of situations you may encounter every day. Others feel that it is nerve-wracking to walk into a high-stakes test without making adequate preparation. There is a balance somewhere in the middle of the two opinions. Of course you can study to some degree. For those who are very nervous about test taking, studying helps to alleviate the pre-test jitters. It helps candidates feel that they have done all they can to test well. It also helps to have some thoughts in mind to get you started writing a response, since you only have thirty minutes per exercise.

It is difficult, however, to know what to study. The best way to study is to scan the six subject areas and prepare a chart similar to a KWL (What you know, want to know, and learned) chart you might use with students, but in this case it will be a K (what you know), W (want to know), and L (list of materials and study guides). For each exercise, list the things you already know well about that subject, then list the things you need to know more about. In the last column, list some books, Web sites, and other materials that might help you prepare.

Assessment Center KWL

Table 34

Exercise 1: Organizational Management

Already Know	Want to Know	Materials/Study Guides

Exercise 2: Ethical and Legal Tenets

Already Know	Want to Know	Materials/Study Guides

Exercise 3: Technologies

Already Know	Want to Know	Materials/Study Guides

Exercise 4: Collection Development

Already Know	Want to Know	Materials/Study Guides

Exercise 5: Information Literacy

Already Know	Want to Know	Materials/Study Guides

Exercise 6: Knowledge of Literature

Already Know	Want to Know	Materials/Study Guides

Helpful Resources for the Online Assessment

Exercise 1: Organizational Management

Web Sites

http://www.oklibs.org/~oaslms/resource_page.htm#OrganizationalManagement

http://backflips.com/members/librarymedia/11786142

Alewine, M. 2005. "School library media specialists: Essentially administrators." *Knowledge Quest* on the Web. Retrieved 4/3/05 from the URL: http://www.ala.org/ala/aasl/aaslpubsandjournals/kqweb/kqarchives/vol32/alewine.htm

American Association of School Librarians. 2005. Position statement on appropriate staffing for school library media centers. Retrieved 4/5/05 from the URL: http://www.ala.org/aasl/aaslproftools/positionstatements/aaslpositionstatementappropriate.htm

American Association of School Librarians. 2005. Position statement on flexible scheduling. Retrieved 4/5/05 from the URL: http://www.ala.org/aasl/aaslproftools/positionstatements/aaslpositionstatement.htm

Starr, L. 2000. "Strong libraries improve student achievement." Retrieved 4/3/05 from the URL: http://www.educationworld.com/a_admin/admin/admin178.shtml

Print Resources

American Association of School Librarians and Association for Educational Communications and Technology. 1998. *Information power: Building partnerships for learning.* American Library Association.

Thelen, L. 2003. *Essentials of elementary school library management.* Kettering, OH: Linworth Publishing, Inc.

Exercise 2: Ethical and Legal Tenets

Web Sites

http://www.oklibs.org/~oaslms/resource_page.htm#Ethics

http://www.backflips.com/members/librarymedia/11786143

http://eduscapes.com/seeds/censor.html

Print Resources

Johnson, D. 2003. *Learning right from wrong in the digital age: An ethics guide for parents, teachers, librarians, and others who care about computer-using young people.* Linworth Publishing, Inc.

Reichman, H. 2001. *Censorship and Selection: issues and answers for schools.* American Library Association.

Simpson, C. 2001. *Copyright for Schools: A practical guide, third edition.* Linworth Publishing, Inc.

Simpson, C. 2003. *Ethics in school librarianship: A reader.* Linworth Publishing, Inc.

Exercise 3: Technologies

Web Sites

http://www.oklibs.org/~oaslms/resource_page.htm#Technologies

http://www.backflips.com/members/librarymedia/11786143

Print Resources

Glandon, S. 2002. *Integrating technology: Effective tools for collaboration.* Linworth Publishing, Inc.

ISTE Nets Standards. Retrieved 4/3/05 from the URL: http://cnets.iste.org/

Exercise 4: Collection Development

Web Sites

http://www.oklibs.org/~oaslms/resource_page.htm#Collection

http://www.coe.ilstu.edu/ilnbpts/NBCT/CertificateSpecificResources/LibraryMedia-ECYA.htm# Exercise_4

Print Resources

Loertscher, D. and Woolls, B. 2004. *Building a school library collection plan.* Hi Willow Research and Publishing.

Van Orden, P. and Bishop, K. 2001. *The collection development program in schools.* Libraries Unlimited.

Exercise 5: Information Literacy

Web Sites

http://www.oklibs.org/~oaslms/resource_page.htm#Literacy

http://www.coe.ilstu.edu/ilnbpts/NBCT/CertificateSpecificResources/LibraryMedia-ECYA.htm# Exercise_5

Print Resources

Eisenberg, M. and Berkowitz, R. 1990. *Information problem-solving:* The Big 6 approach to library and information skills instruction. Linworth Publishing, Inc.

Exercise 6: Knowledge of Literature

Web Sites

http://www.oklibs.org/~oaslms/resource_page.htm#Literature

Print Resources

Ayers, L. 2003. *Read it again! Standards-based literature lessons for young children.* Linworth Publishing, Inc.

Bishop, K. 2003. *Connecting libraries with classrooms: The curricular roles of the media specialist.* Linworth Publishing, Inc.

Loertscher, D. and Woolls, B. 2002. *Information literacy: a review of the research.* Hi Willow Research and Publishing.

Miller, D. 2004. *The Standards-based integrated library: A collaborative approach for aligning the library program with the classroom curriculum.* Linworth Publishing, Inc.

Obert, B. and Barr, P. 2004. *Capturing readers with children's choice book awards: A directory of state programs.*

Public Education Network and American Association of School Librarians. 2001. "The Information-powered school." American Library Association.

Chapter Fourteen

AFTER SCORES ARE ANNOUNCED, *Then What?*

CHAPTER FOURTEEN AT A GLANCE
- **Journal Entry: November 23** 138
- When Will Scores Be Announced? 139
- Suppose a Candidate Does Not Achieve Certification? 139
- **Journal Entry: November 30** 140
- Benefits of Achieving National Board Certification 141
- **Journal Entry: September 2** 142
- Educational Honor Society 141
- **Journal Entry: November 15** 143
- Continued Professional Growth 141
- Ethics for NBCTs 144

November 23

It is almost Thanksgiving and I am numb with anticipation. I feel that I did well on my portfolio entries, but I am uncertain about my online assessment performance. I have never been a good test taker, and I was especially nervous during this test. I was well prepared for the exercises but I know that I forgot a few things I had prepared to use once I began writing. I hope that overall I did well enough to obtain certification. And, I really hope the scores are posted before the Thanksgiving break. I have heard that they might be. I am so tired of waiting to see the results. I am going to check every day until then to see if our scores have been posted.

> *"If you're lucky enough to do well,*
> *it's your responsibility to send the elevator back down."*
> —Kevin Spacey

When Will Scores Be Announced?

All scoring is done at designated assessment centers over the summer months when assessors, who are practicing teachers themselves, are available to score. Verification of scores, electronic compiling of scores, totaling each candidate's scores, and late scoring is completed in the fall. Score reports become available to candidates generally between the week before Thanksgiving and the end of December.

The National Board for Professional Teaching Standards takes pride in the high degree of validity and reliability of its scoring process. The scoring system was developed by the Educational Testing Service, Inc. and is monitored by ETS and Harcourt Educational Measurement. The National Board continuously evaluates its assessments and the assessment process to ensure it is fair and consistent and that the scoring of candidate entries is both reliable and accurate.

Suppose a Candidate Does Not Achieve Certification?

Scores are announced online initially and then are submitted to government reporting agencies. Candidates may login to the NBRIC http://www.nbpts.org/candidates/scorereporting.cfm to obtain their official score report.

All individual scores of 2.75 or better are considered accomplished. The National Board will automatically bank scores lower than 2.75 for any candidate who does not achieve certification on their initial attempt. Candidates may than reattempt to achieve certification over a 24-month period following the date of their initial score report. Candidates may retake each portfolio entry or assessment center exercise up to two times during the 24-month period that scores are banked, but retake scores will always replace initial scores, whether higher or lower. Each retake item costs $350 and fees for retake items are nonrefundable. All portfolio entry work must be completely new, although some of the same accomplishments may be submitted for Portfolio Entry 4.

Fast Fact:
Learn more about score banking and retakes at **http://www.nbpts.org/candidates/scorebankretake.cfm**.

Candidates with a high number of retakes may find it easier and less expensive to begin all over again to attempt certification. Whatever a candidate decides, he or she should be aware that the certification process for many individuals takes up to three years. And every candidate should realize

November 30

Wow! I made it! I am so relieved! I agonized for so many months and then had to wait while I worried and wondered if what I did was good enough to earn certification. Now all that hard work can really pay off.

I am delighted that now I can earn a state pay raise. And, I found out that my state will reimburse my expenses!

Of course I am inspired to help others now. I wonder, what other benefits are out there for NBCTs? I am going to investigate opportunities for NBCTs locally and see what I might be qualified to do.

that an accomplished individual may not achieve certification for lack of following directions or not supplying enough detail to be "clear, consistent, and convincing." The process of detailing, analyzing, and reflecting on one's practice by creating a professional portfolio for many candidates is a new and daunting experience, and that in itself is quite an accomplishment. Candidacy is a tremendous professional growth experience, and all candidates benefit from it whether they achieve certification on their initial attempt or not. Most would agree, however, that the rigorous expectations and high stakes involved in the process are what make certification so prestigious and rewarding to accomplish.

Benefits of Achieving National Board Certification

The candidates who do achieve certification find there are many benefits beyond the initial exhilaration of having attained the required 275 points on the score report. Many districts offer their National Board Certified Teachers (NBCTs) a bonus check, and many states offer a salary supplement to NBCTs for the life of their certificate. In addition, a variety of states reimburse expenses occurred in obtaining certification, and the majority of states guarantee portability of licensing from state to state. As of this writing, legislation has been enacted in all 50 states and around 544 school districts to recognize and reward NBCTs.

Fast Fact:
*Find out more about state and district incentives at **http://www.nbpts.org/about/state.cfm**.*

In addition to public recognition and monetary incentives, a variety of colleges and universities offer graduate credit to NBCTs. For a small fee, NBCTs can apply to the American Council for Education (ACE) for a transcript reflecting the number of graduate credit hours they recommend. NBCTs can then submit this transcript to a college, university, state department or local school district to be considered for credit toward degree programs, license renewal, salary stipends, or staff development hours. ACE recommends that teachers who attempt National Board Certification receive up to three semester hours of graduate credit for completing the process and an additional three hours for achieving certification.

Educational Honor Society

Pi Lambda Theta, an International Honor Society and Professional Educational Association invites all NBCTs into its membership whether or not they have attained the qualifications for membership. More information on membership can be obtained online at http://www.pilambda.org/nbpts.html.

Continued Professional Growth

In addition, many NBCTs desire to continue growing professionally and reaching out to others. The National Board hosts an annual conference and NBCTs are encouraged to come together to meet others, share ideas, and renew their passion to build stronger learning communities and for better teaching. Many states offer their own state conferences, as well. More information about the national conference can be obtained online at www.nbpts.org/events/conference.cfm.

September 2

It is a new school year. I have received my official certificate from the National Board (I have framed it and put it on the wall in my office). Last December, I was notified of my state pay raise. Over the summer I had a chance to reflect on the intense activities of the previous year and I feel more comfortable and reassured of my accomplishment and ways that I can make a difference.

Today something interesting came in the mail: it was an invitation to join an honor society—Pi Lambda Theta. Apparently, all NBCTs are invited to join as certification is considered equal to meeting all requirements for membership.

November 15

Today I visited the National Board Web site to check for the announcement of new NBCTs and read about the National Conference. I had attended my state conference and met many other NBCTs statewide, particularly some NBC media specialists. It is good to stay connected with others as media specialists tend to be somewhat isolated in their jobs. I am keeping track of all these e-mail addresses so we can communicate throughout the year.

Now I am thinking that I may see if another NBC media specialist in my district would be interested in presenting at the National Conference with me. We have a couple of projects going in our district that might be of interest on a national scale. I hope I can talk her into helping me submit an application online. The deadline is December 15.

Outreach is a rewarding way to make a difference locally. Many NBCTs find that mentoring others is very satisfying and helps to restore their commitment to the profession. Others find that speaking to groups such as business partners and government organizations about the benefits of hiring National Board Certified Teachers is fulfilling. The National Board for Professional Teaching Standards offers a variety of tools to assist with advocacy, including publications and videos as well as training tools.

Fast fact:

Find out more about the National Board's advocacy tools online at http://www.nbpts.org/events/products.cfm, http://www.nbpts.org/edreform/index.cfm, and http://www.nbpts.org/about/govt.cfm.

Some NBCTs may wish to work as assessors, facilitate courses or academies for candidates, or join teacher leadership initiatives such as those supported by State Farm and the Association for Supervision and Curriculum Development. The ASCD has partnered with the National Board to invite NBCTs to create videos, submit conference proposals, or apply to become a member of the Professional Development Institute or ASCD faculty. NBCTs can apply online at http://www.nbpts.org/pdf/ascd_opp_app.pdf. State Farm has created a liaison program to utilize NBCTs in speaking to businesses about the benefits of National Board Certification. For more information or to apply online visit http://www.nbpts.org/nbct/sf.cfm.

Fast Fact:

More information about teacher leadership initiatives is available online at http://www.nbpts.org/nbct/for.cfm and http://www.nbpts.org/nbct/lead.cfmn.

Ethics for NBCTs

The National Board for Professional Teaching Standards has established a policy regarding the use of its copyrighted materials for noncommercial, educational purposes provided 1) the materials protect the confidentiality of individuals and organizations participating in the National Board Certification process, 2) the access complies with the National Board's policies and contractual agreements, and 3) the access provides no financial loss to the National Board for Professional Teaching Standards, and may, in fact, produce revenue. National Board Certified Teachers may request permission to use publications, videos, software, and multimedia products for educational purposes only. Actual candidate responses from NBCTs and veteran candidates may be used with permission. National Board trademarks and logos may be used with permission. Scores and statistics may be obtained for research purposes only. More information about ethics for NBCTs is available at http://www.nbpt.org/pdf/policy_ethical_cand_supp.pdf

All NBCTs will no doubt continue to grow professionally and to serve their staff, students, and community with accomplished teaching. Hopefully, a number of NBCTs will seek opportunities to serve where their special skills are needed most to improve teaching and learning nationwide.

Appendices

Appendix A
Peggy's Personal Glossary of Terms for National Board Candidates

Accomplishment: Reflecting the vision of practice which incorporates the five core propositions and the ten benchmarks for library media specialists

Advocacy: Activities which promote National Board certification and educate the public about the advantages of having National Board Certified teachers on staff

Analytical writing: Writing which explains the rationale for a particular methodology, activity, or lesson plan incorporated into classroom practice; answers the question, why?

Architecture of Accomplishment: The structural model or design that signifies exemplary instructional practices and results in outstanding student achievement

Articulate: To verbalize or put into words ideas, thoughts, and feelings about one's practice; to explain in detail

Assessment Center: A designated site for online assessment pre-approved by the National Board for Professional Teaching Standards

Assessor: A certified teacher practicing in a National Board certificate field who has been rigorously trained to score candidate entries in accordance with the National Board standards, benchmarks, and rubrics

Benchmark: A point of reference or standard against which candidate entries may be evaluated; a scale for measuring performance

Bias: A prejudice or preconceived notion consciously or unconsciously held by an individual; all assessors are trained to identify and suppress any biases they may have while scoring

Candidate: A certified teacher who has applied for and been accepted as a contender for National Board Certification

Certificate field: A teaching field recognized with its own portfolio requirements and assessment center exercises and certifiable by the National Board for Professional Teaching Standards

Certification: An award presented to a candidate who has successfully scored a total of 275 or more points

Collaboration: A cooperative partnership with another teacher; teamwork

Community: Adults and other partners in a particular area or field of interest who share a common bond, such as the achievement of the students at the local school

Connections: Links a student makes between a piece of literature and his or her own experience, other pieces of literature, or life itself; a strategy for strengthening literature comprehension

Descriptive writing: Writing which explains the demographic and geographic statistics and definitive characteristics of a particular group as well as the details of a particular activity of that group; answers the questions, who and how?

Entry: A response or submission, such as a candidate's portfolio entry

Exercise: A task or essay a candidate is expected to complete for the online assessment

Evidence: A variety of types of documentation such as student work samples, videotapes, certificates, letters from parents, coworkers, and administrators, awards, graduate degrees, publications, and so on that indicate contributions to the field of education and to student achievement

Facilitator: An individual who oversees the activities of another individual or group of individuals with similar interests, goals, and beliefs

Intellectual property: Copyrighted work of an individual

Instructional context: Relevant information that frames a teaching situation with an individual group of students at a particular time in a specific place

Licensing: State requirements for obtaining a teaching certificate

Mentor: An experienced guide who can assist a candidate through his or her candidacy

Overarching statement: Defining statement that identifies the key elements of a response; used in the rubric to identify the significant parts of a response

Pan: A 360o sweep of an area showing all four corners and walls from floor to ceiling

Portfolio: A compilation of student work samples, written commentary, videotapes, and selected documents representing a teacher's practice

Practice: The daily routines and modes of operation a teacher uses to plan, implement, and assess her instruction

Prompt: A trigger to stimulate a response, as in the scenario described for the online assessment exercises

Propositions: The five core beliefs concerning what accomplished teachers should know and be able to do

Reflection: Introspective examination of one's own practice to identify and improve on weaknesses while fostering strengths

Reflective writing: Writing that explains the process of thinking about one's practice and how to improve it

Rubric: A set of rules for scoring that describe the essential qualities of performance; for National Board, the rubrics were carefully selected and reviewed to precisely describe distinctions of performance on four levels

Scoring guide: Written set of rules and tools used to determine levels of candidate performance

Standards: The benchmarks representing a consensus from experts in the field of the essential knowledge, skills, and practices that represent accomplishment

Technologies: All types of electronic equipment including but not limited to computers, printers, videocassette players and recorders, audiocassette players and recorders, cameras, camcorders, PDAs, calculators, projectors, whiteboards, scanners, and other peripherals

Tenet: A principal or underlying belief; a precept

Unedited: Continuous segment that is uninterrupted and not manipulated in any way to vary from its original form

Appendix B

Resource List

Accomplished Teacher Magazine	www.nbpts.org/nbct/atmag.cfm
Advocacy Tools	www.nbpts.org/events/products.cfm
	www.nbpts.org/about/govt.cfm
American Library Association	www.ala.org
ASCD for NBCTs	www.nbpts.org/pdf/ascd_opp_app.pdf
Assessment Center Orientation	www.nbpts.org/candidates/acob
Assessor Qualifications	www.nbpts.org/standards/assessors.cfm
California Arts Project Videotaping Guide	http://csmp.ucop.edu/tcap/nbpts/tutorials/video.html
Candidate Fees	www.nbpts.org/candidates/guide/4_feecht.html
Candidate Loans	www.neamb.com/loans/loanbc.jsp
Candidate Profile	www.nbpts.org/myprofile
Candidate Scoring Guide	www.nbpts.org/candidates/scoringguides.cfm
Carnegie Task Force	www.nbpts.org/about/hist.cfm#taskforce
Collaborative Lesson Plans	www.education-world.com/a_lesson
Current NBCTs	www.nbpts.org/nbct/nbctdir_byyear.cfm

Documenting Accomplishments	www.nbpts.org/candidates/guide/04port/04_ecyalm_instructions/04_ecya_lm_entry4.pdf
Five Core Propositions	www.nbpts.org/about/coreprops.cfm
Graduate Credit	https://survey2000.nbpts.org/ace/begin.cfm
In Focus Videotaping Guide	www.focusinfo.com/support/articles/vedit.htm
Leadership Initiatives	www.nbpts.org/nbct/for.cfm
	www.nbpts.org/nbct/lead.cfm
Library Media Portfolio Requirements	www.nbpts.org/candidates/guide/04port/04_ecya_lm.html
Library Media Standards	www.nbpts.org/candidates/guide/whichcert/24EarlychildYoungLibMedia.html
Mission of the National Board	www.nbpts.org/about/hist.cfm
National Board Conference	http://www.nbpts.org/events/conference.cfm
National Board Constitution	nbpts.org/about/dir.cfm
National Board Vision for Accomplished Teaching	www.nbpts.org/standards/nbcert.cfm#stdgeninfo
National Education Association Candidate's Guidebook	www.nea.org/nationalboard/images/2005-nbc-guide.pdf
National Education Association Writing Matrix	www.nea.org/nationalboard/images/2005-nbc-Chpt6.pdf
NBPTS Promotional Videos	www.nbpts.org/news/tv_news.cfm
NCSS Thematic Standards	www.ncess.org/standards/teachers/programmatic.1.html
Online News	www.nbpts.org/news/tv_news.cfm
Pi Lambda Theta Society	www.pilambda.org/nbpts.html
Practice Online Assessment	www.nbpts.org/candidates/tutorial.cfm
Professional Standards Newsletter	www.nbpts.org/events/theprofessionalstandard.cfm
Qualifications of Candidacy	www.nbpts.org/candidates/index.cfm#2
Retakes	www.nbpts.org/candidates/scorebankretake.cfm
Scholarship Information	www.nbpts.org/candidates/availscholar.cfm
School Library Journal Online	www.slj.com
Score Reports	www.nbpts.org/candidates/scorereporting.cfm
State Farm Liaison Program	www.nbpts.org/nbct/sf.cfm
State Incentives	www.nbpts.org/about/state.cfm
Video Clips of NBCTs	www.nbpts.org/highered/digitaledge.cfm
Yahoo Groups Library Media list-serve	http://groups.yahoo.com/group/librarymedia/

Index

A

Accomplished
    Library Media Specialist 41
    Teacher Magazine 59
Accomplishment
    evidence 25
    definition 41, 146
Analyzing
    student work 98
Assessment
    tips 73
    overview 75
    what matters 75
    tips 81
Assessors
    qualifications 77
    training 79
    incentives 79
    definition 146
Avedon, Richard (quote) 63

B

Brin, Sergey quote 111

C

Camus, Albert (quote) 57
Candidacy . . . .
    applying 59
Candidate . . . .
    qualifications 15
    definition 146
Capozzi, John (quote) 9
Carnegie Task Force 13
Certification
    benefits 141
    definition 146
Clemmer, Jim (quote) 31
Collaboration
    instructional 91, 93
    documenting 97
    reflection 99
    definition 146
Collaborative
    planning sheet 98
Community Interactions
    log 46
Confucius (quote) 85

D

Dickinson, Emily (quote) .103

E

Entry 1
    resources 99
    rubric 100
    standards 95
Entry 2
    standards 103
    what counts 103
    brainstorming 105
    helpful resources 106
    rubric 107
Entry 3
    standards 111
    what counts 111
    brainstorming 113, 115
    helpful resources 115
    rubric 116
Entry 4
    standards 119
    what counts 119
    brainstorming 121
    documents 123
    description 123
    analysis 123
    resources 124
    rubric 125
    reflection 123
Ethics
    NBCTs 144
Evidence
    documentation 25
    definition 146
Exemplary
    units 85

F

Financial
    information 58
Five Core Propositions 15, 16, 29, 33-37

H

Helpful Web Sites 27
Herbster, Dr. Ben (quote) 49
Honor Society . . . .
    Pi Lambda Theta 141

I

Incentives
    state-based 57

K
Knobel, Stephanie (quote) 13

L
Library Media Specialist
    accomplished 41
Library Media Standards 16, 21, 39, 44-45, 46
Literature
    appreciation of 101
Litwiller, Terry (quote) 129
Lynn, Loretta (quote) 75

N
Nation Prepared
    report 13
National Board
    origin 13
    organization 13
    vision 15
    mission 31
    reform movement 31
    influence 31
    academies 58
    e-mail lists 58
    publications 58
    videos 59
NBCTs by state 33

O
Online Assessment 127
    center KWL 132
    resources 133-135
    center 129, 146
Overview 49

P
Pi Lambda Theta
honor society 141
Player, Gary (quote) 41
Portfolio
    organization 51
    writing styles 83
    instructions 85
    definition 147
Professional growth 141
Proofreaders
    list 57
Propositions
    definition 147

R
Reflection
    definition 147
Reflective practice 25
Rubric
    definition 147

S
Schedule
    events 53
Scores
    announcement 139
Scoring
    rubrics 80
    estimation 80
Scoring guide
    definition 147
Spacey, Kevin (quote) 139
Standards
    definition 147
Support
    obtaining 55
    online 59

T
Time
    commitment 49
Timesaving
    tips 51

V
Videotapes 61
    general requirements 63
    quality 63
    seating students 65
    lighting 65
    sound 65
    tips 67
    self-scoring 71

W
Walton, Sam (quote) 93
Winfrey, Oprah (quote) 119
Writing
    styles 85, 89
    analytical 87, 146
    descriptive 87, 146
    tips 87, 89-90
    reflective 89
    reflective, definition 147

www.ingramcontent.com/pod-product-compliance
Lightning Source LLC
Chambersburg PA
CBHW081828300426
44116CB00014B/2506